pierangelo filigheddu

TASTING THE WORLD
my best pictures

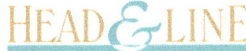

@2022 Pierangelo Filigheddu

≈ redazione editoriale e impaginazione:
  Head&Line

≈ 1ª di copertina:
  Sulla feluca
  Aswan, 2001
  Olympus C3030Z

≈ 4ª di copertina:
  Monument Valley
  USA, 2013
  Apple iPhone 5

≈ ISBN 979-8-3676-9329-4

≈ rev. 4

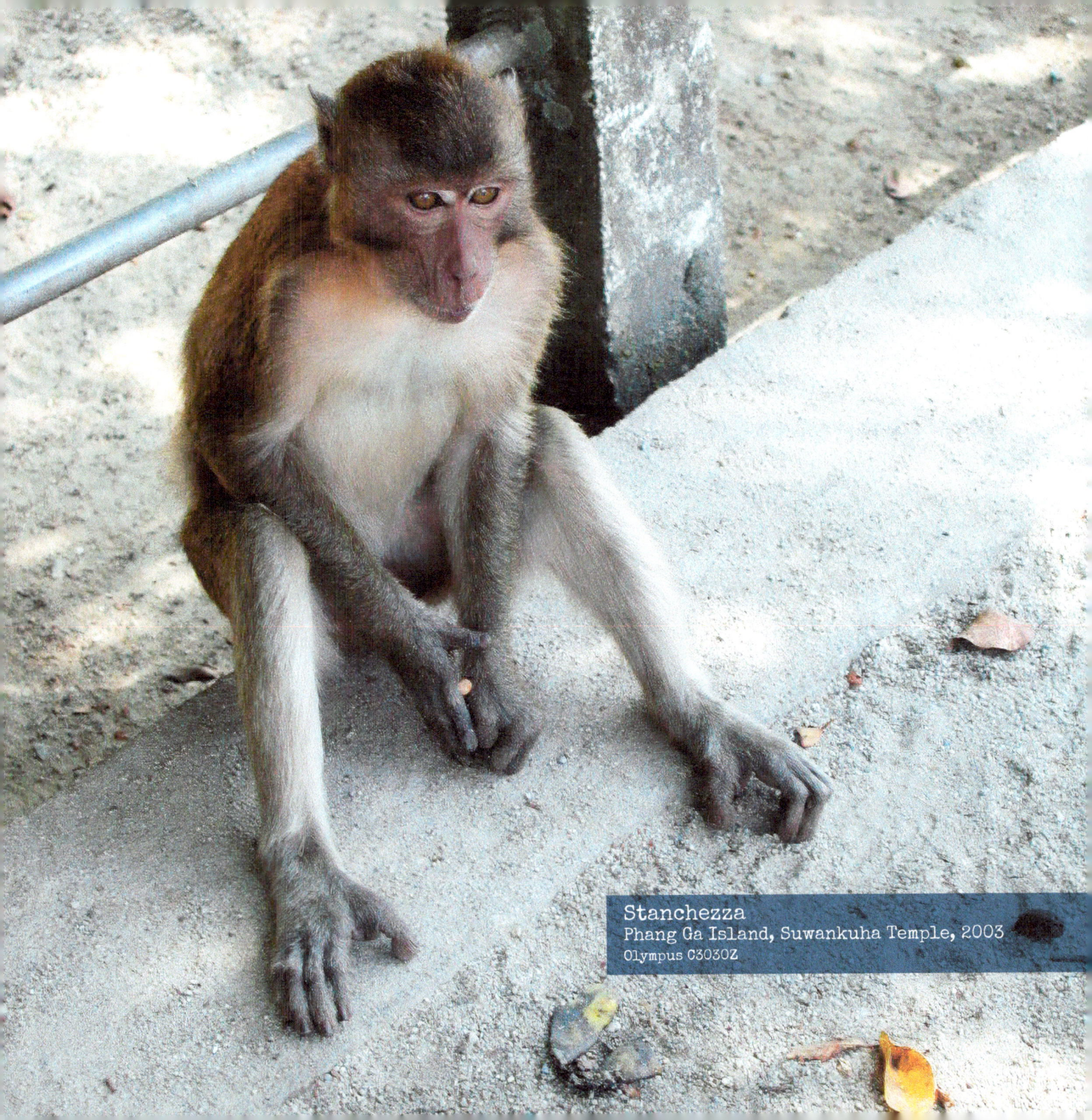

Stanchezza
Phang Ga Island, Suwankuha Temple, 2003
Olympus C3030Z

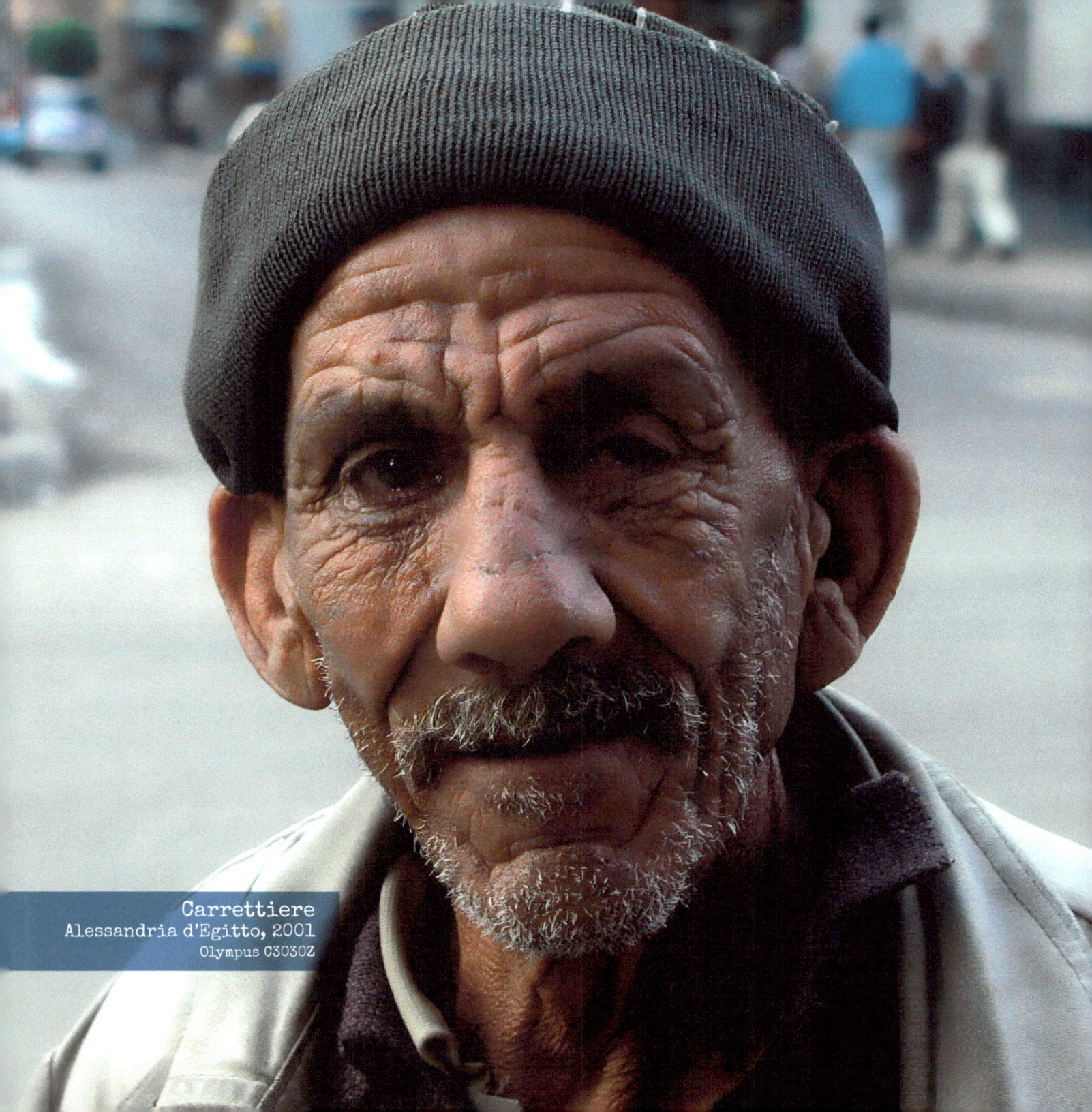

Carrettiere
Alessandria d'Egitto, 2001
Olympus C3030Z

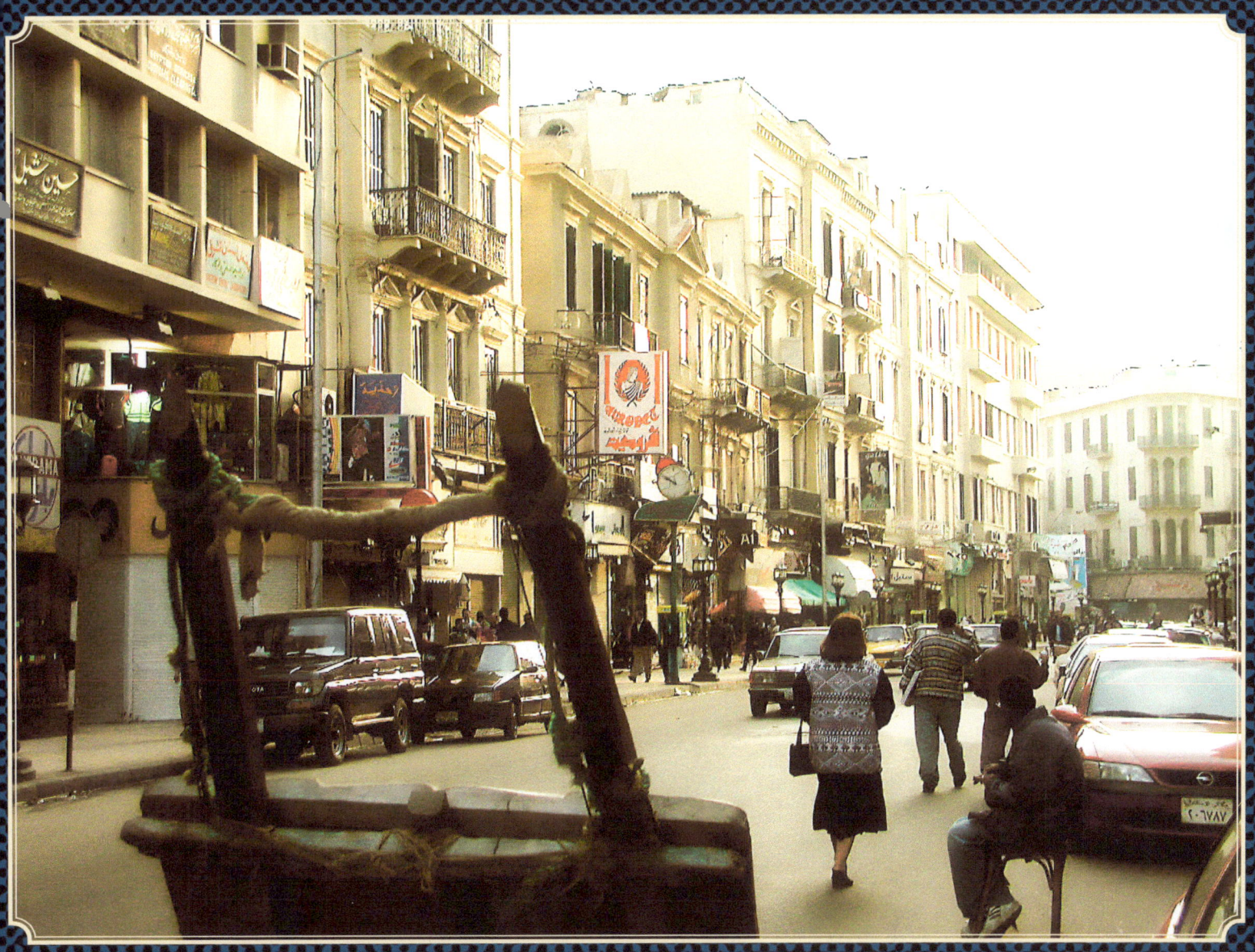

Saad Zaghloul
Alessandria d'Egitto, 2001
Olympus C3030Z

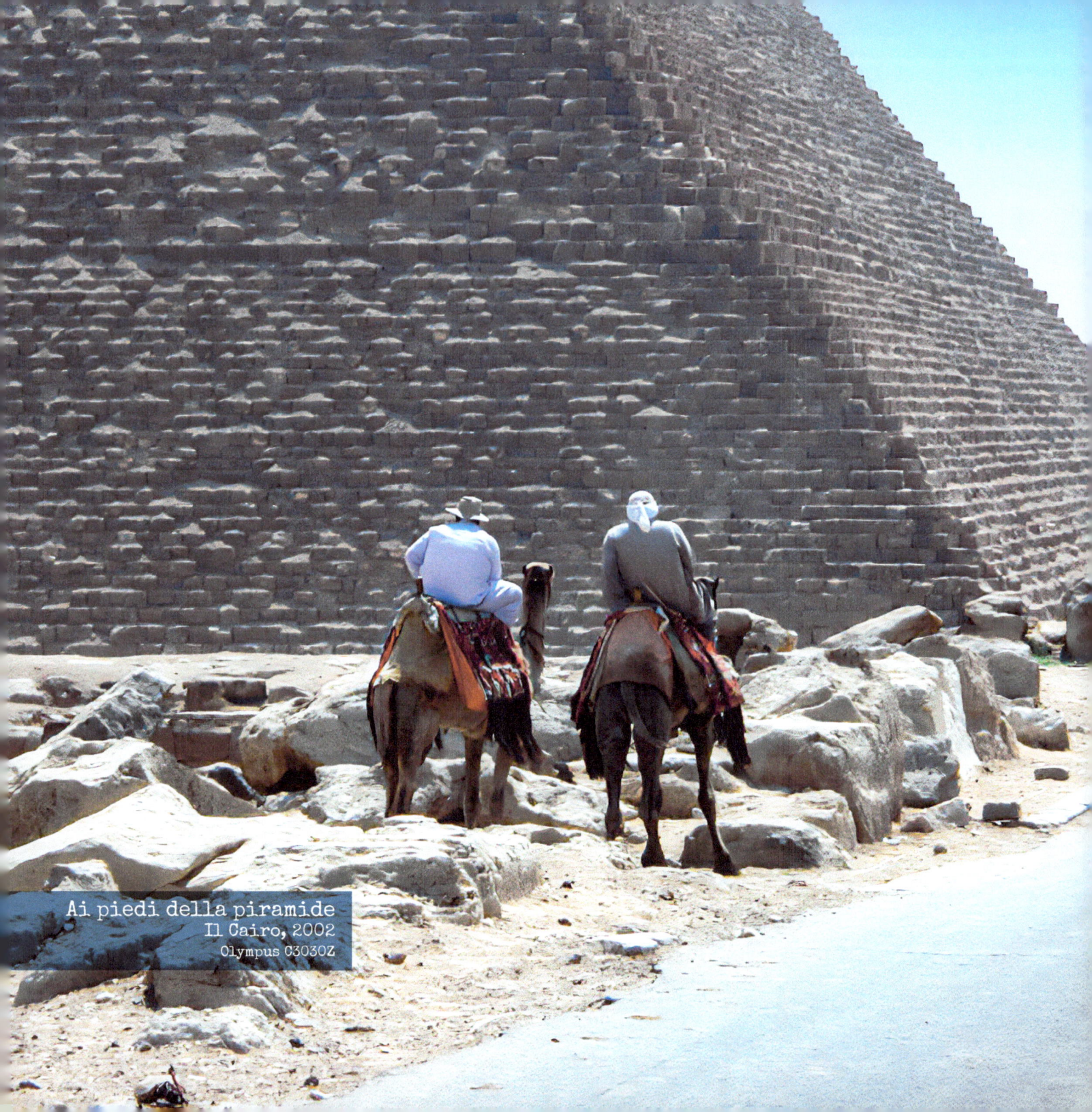

Ai piedi della piramide
Il Cairo, 2002
Olympus C3030Z

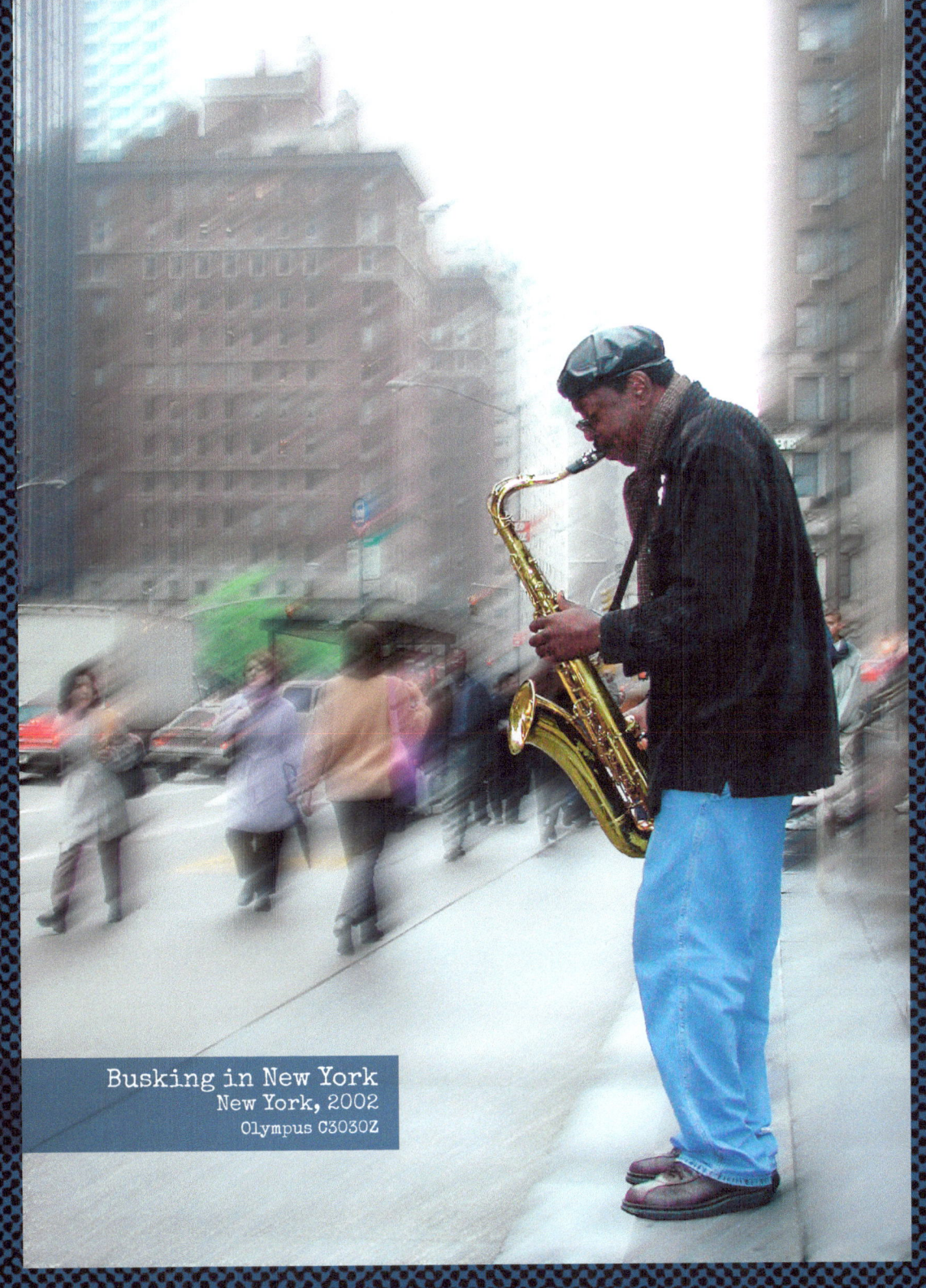

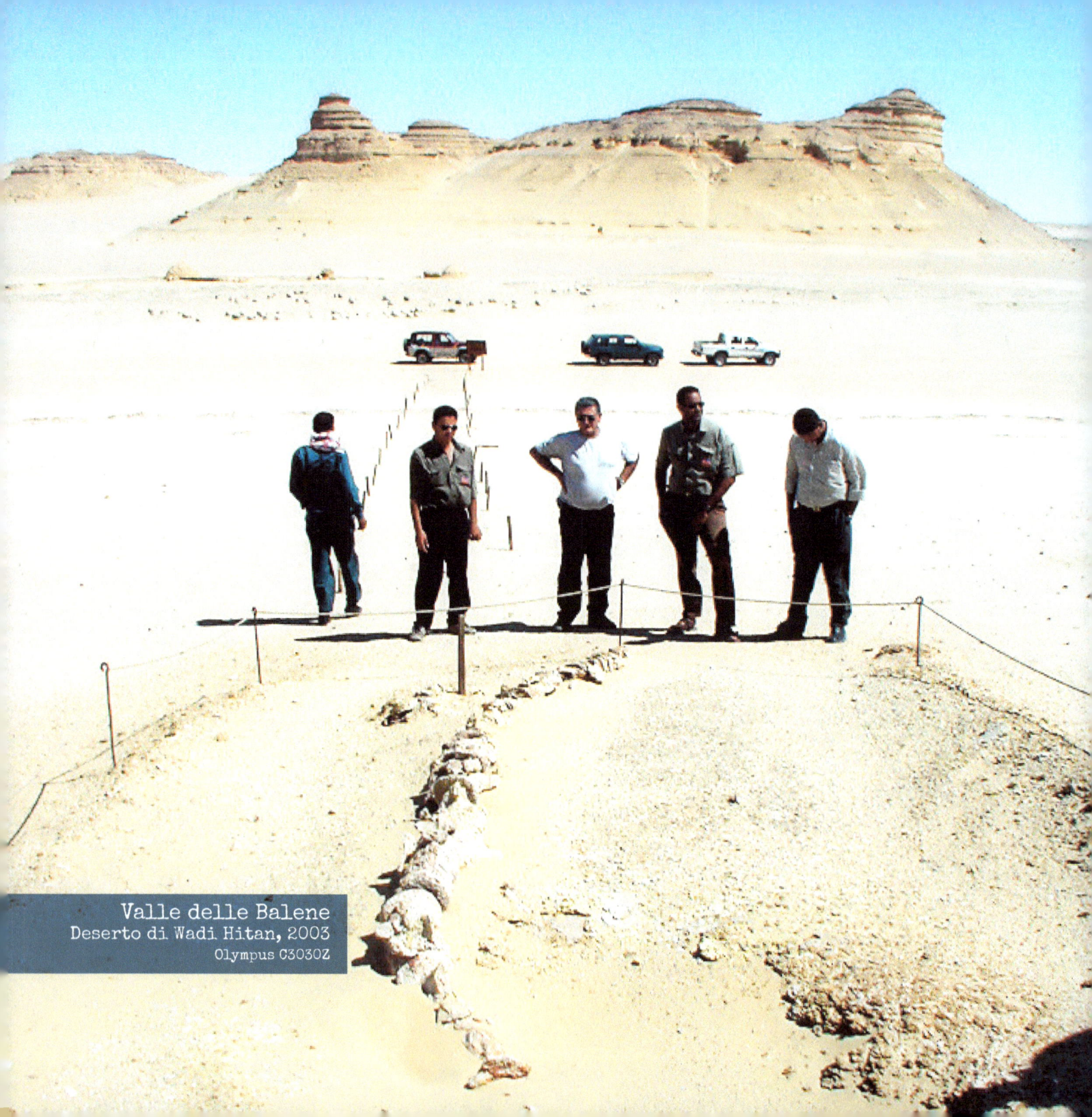

Valle delle Balene
Deserto di Wadi Hitan, 2003
Olympus C3030Z

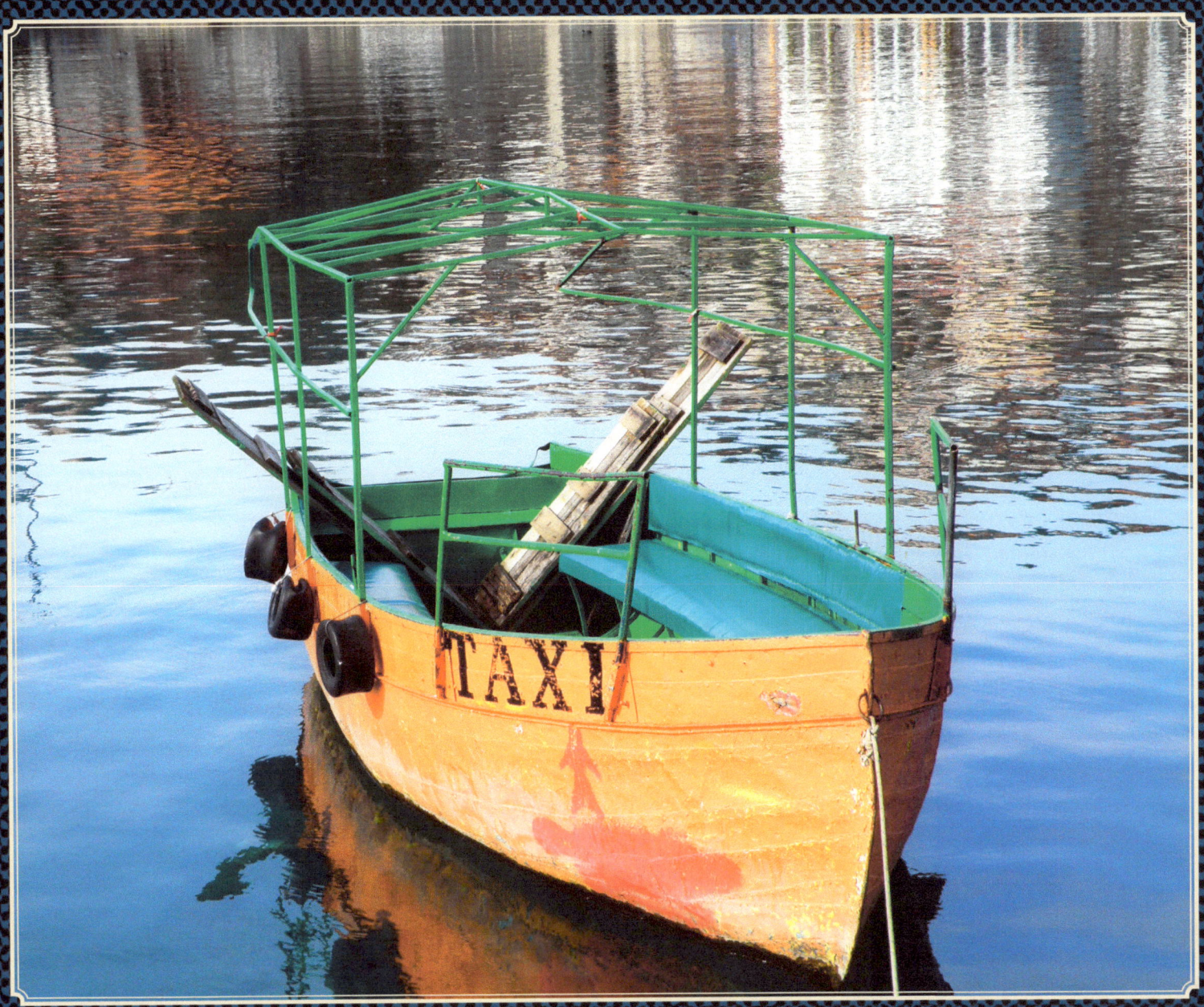

Senza fretta
Ohrid, 2009
Olympus SP565UZ

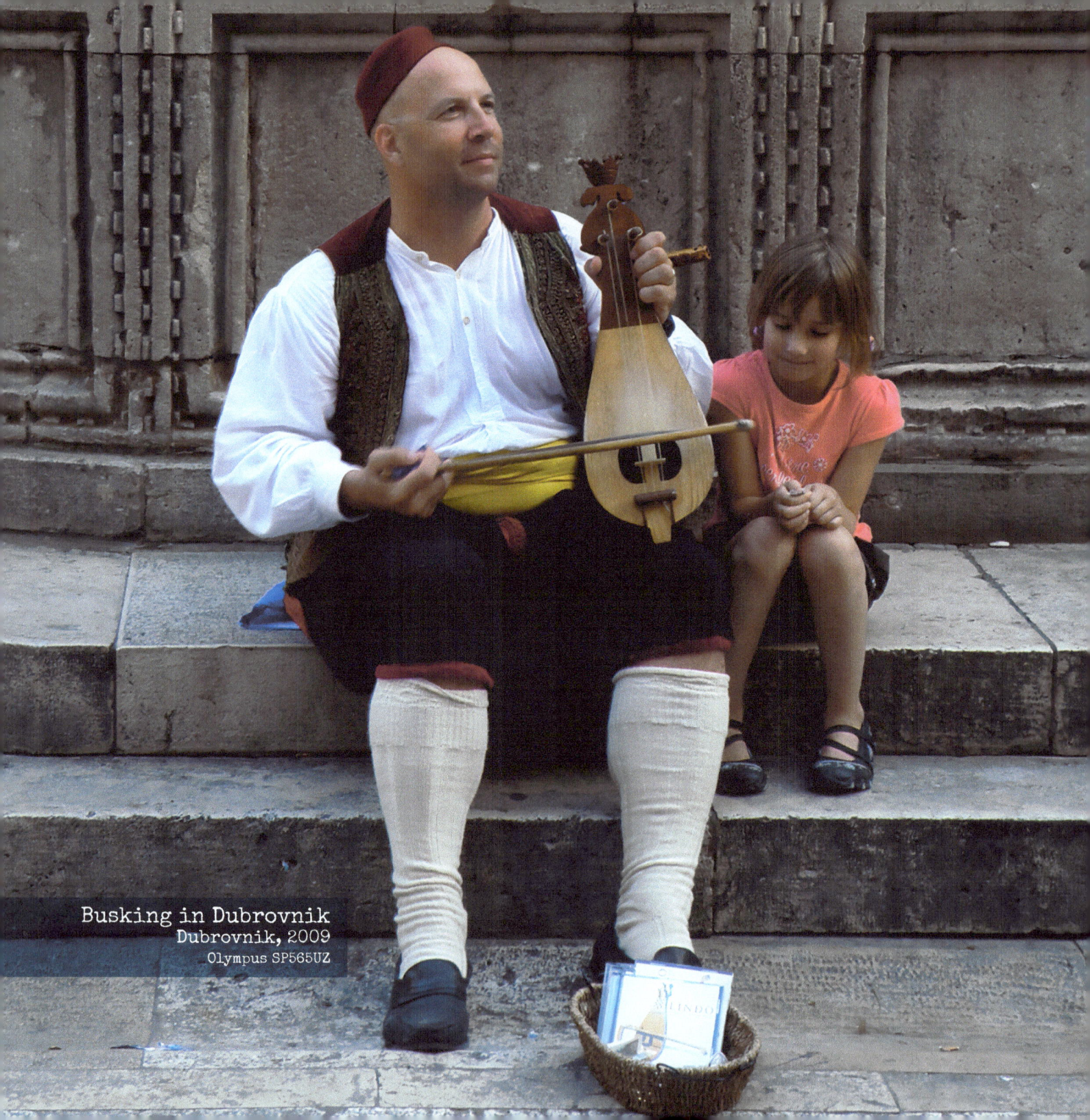

Busking in Dubrovnik
Dubrovnik, 2009
Olympus SP565UZ

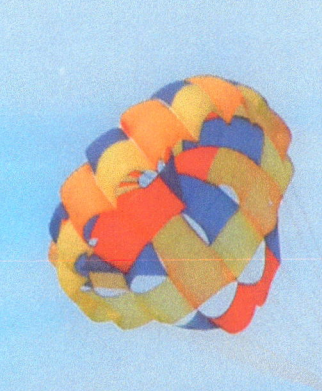

Nei cieli di Punta Cana
Santo Domingo, 2010
Olympus SP565UZ

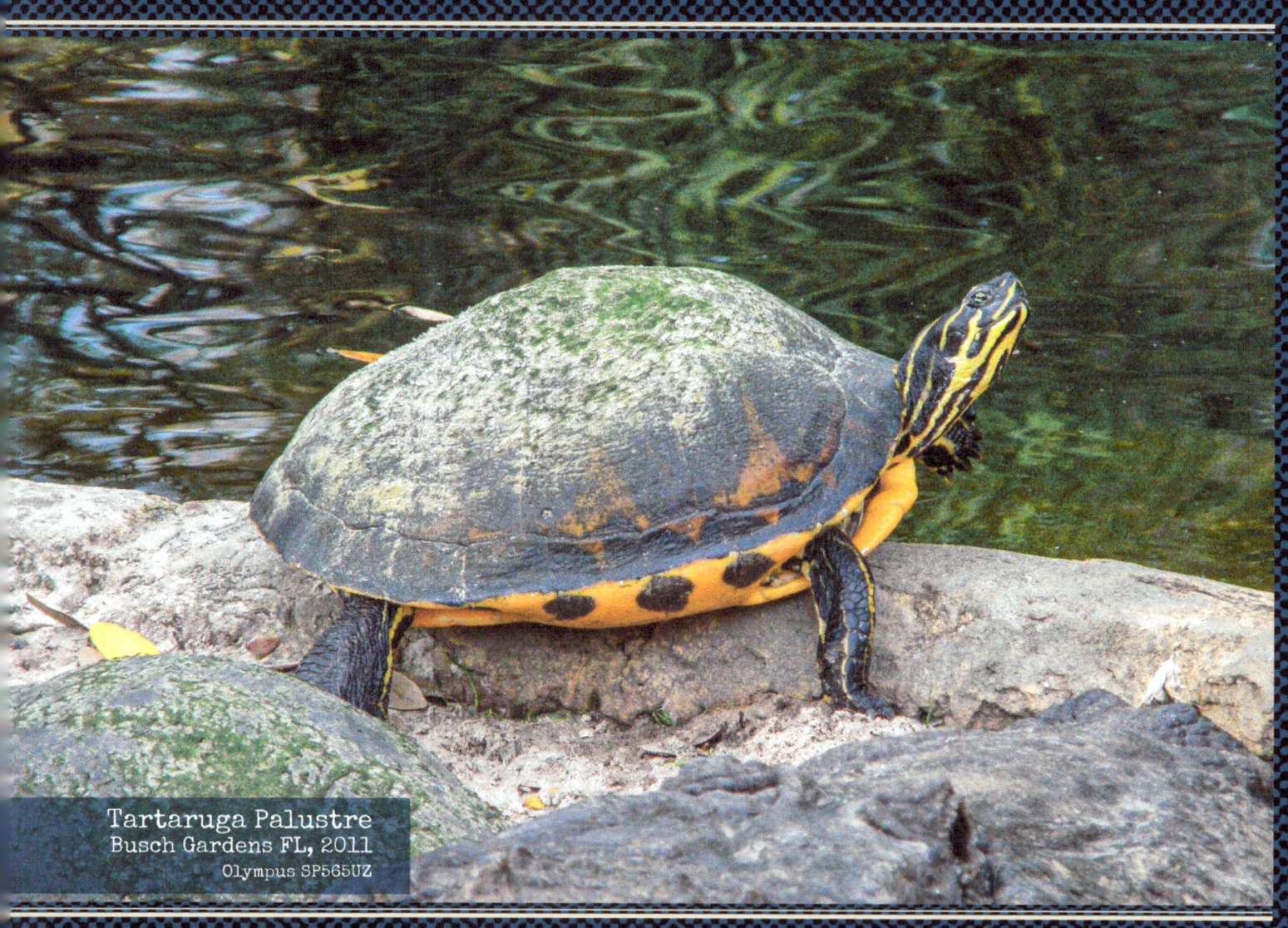

Tartaruga Palustre
Busch Gardens FL, 2011
Olympus SP565UZ

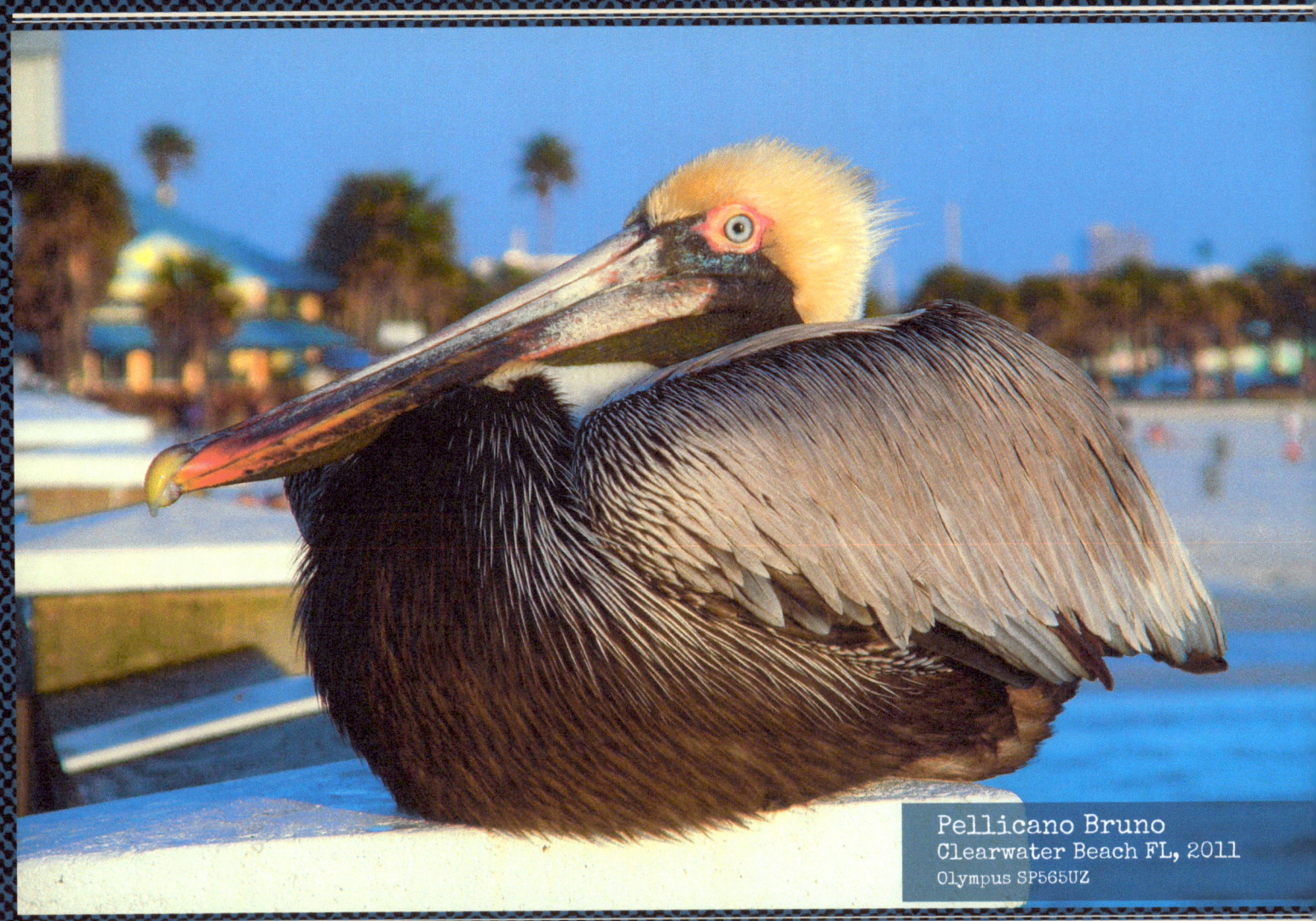

Pellicano Bruno
Clearwater Beach FL, 2011
Olympus SP565UZ

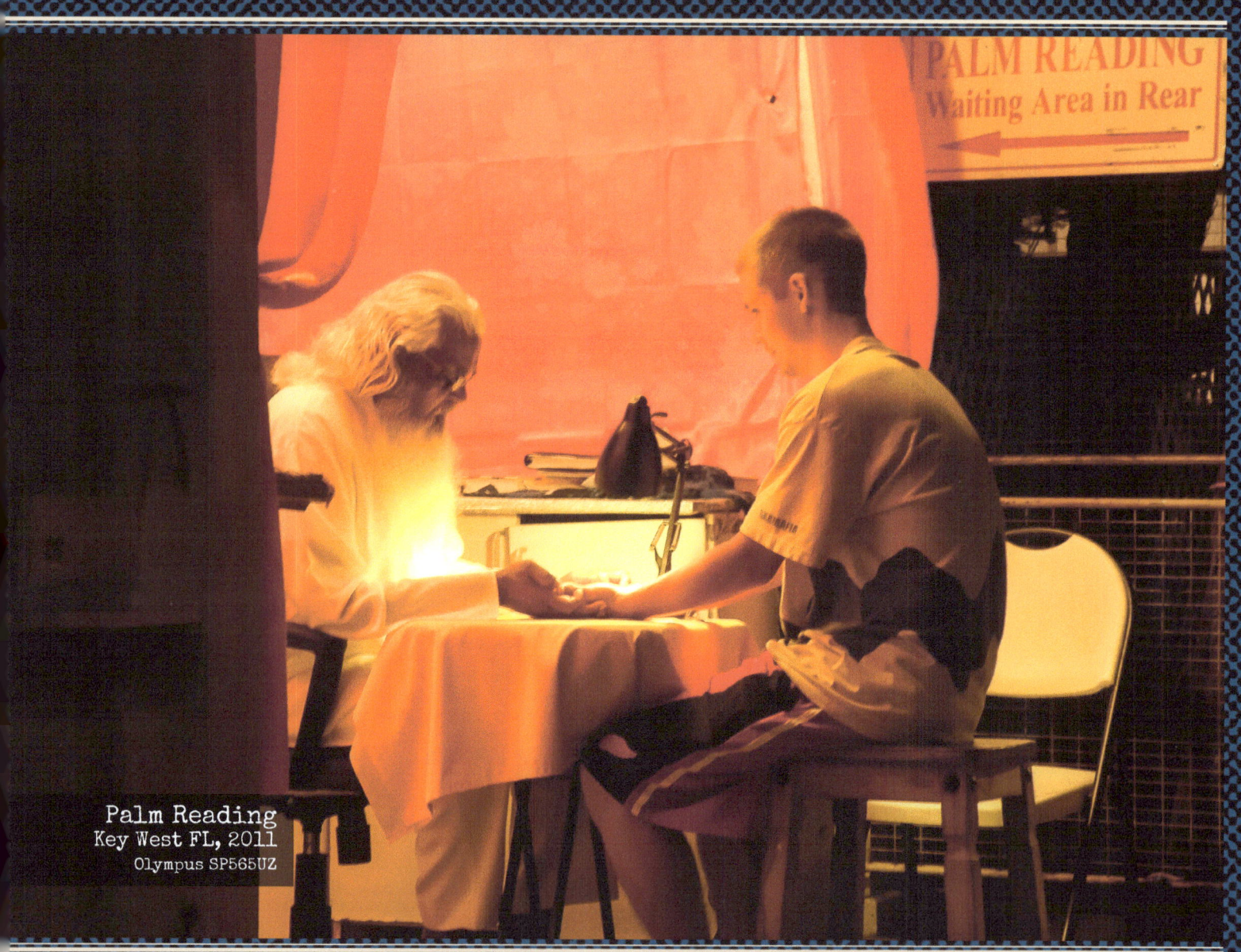

Palm Reading
Key West FL, 2011
Olympus SP565UZ

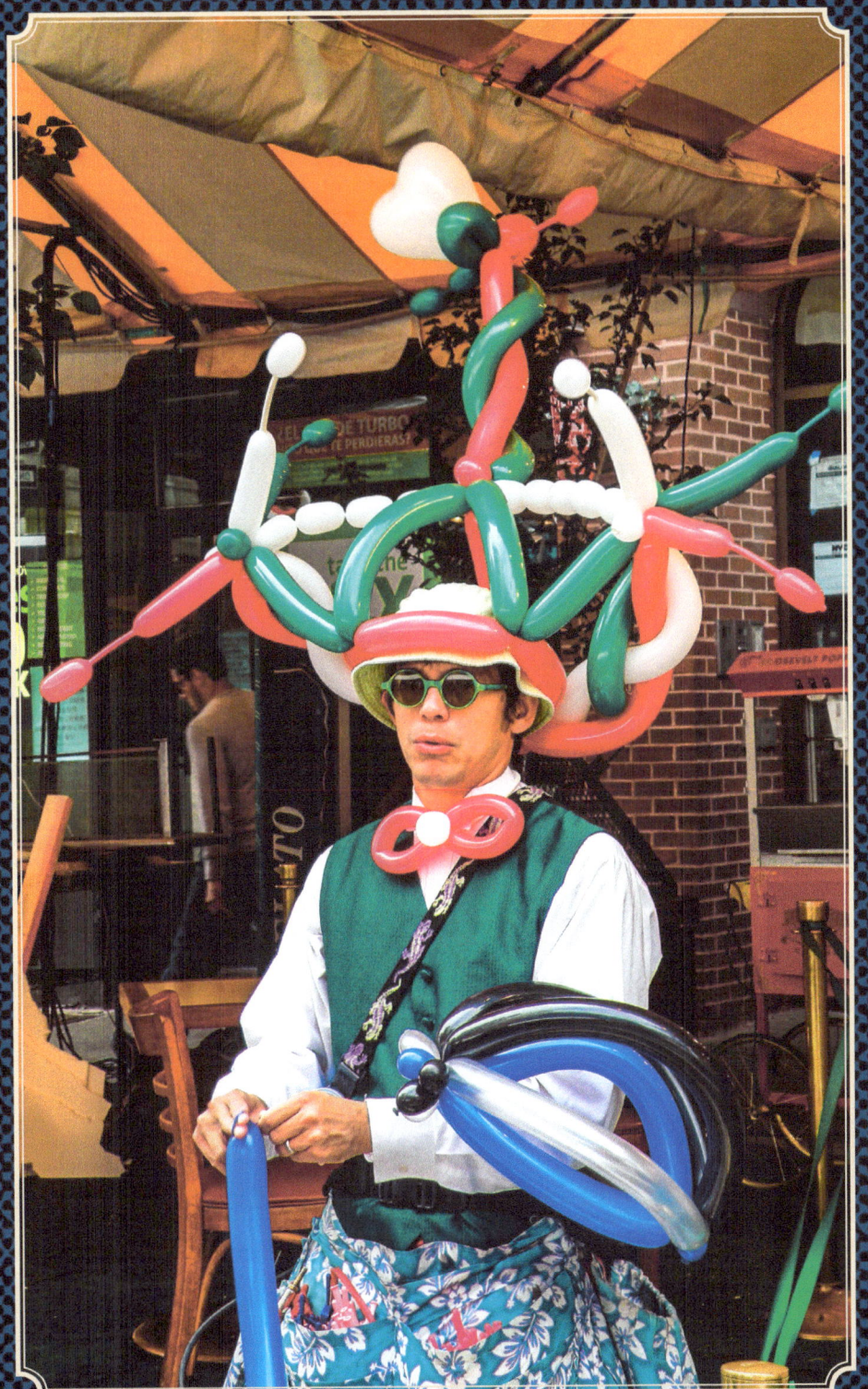

Little Italy
New York, 2011
Olympus SP565UZ

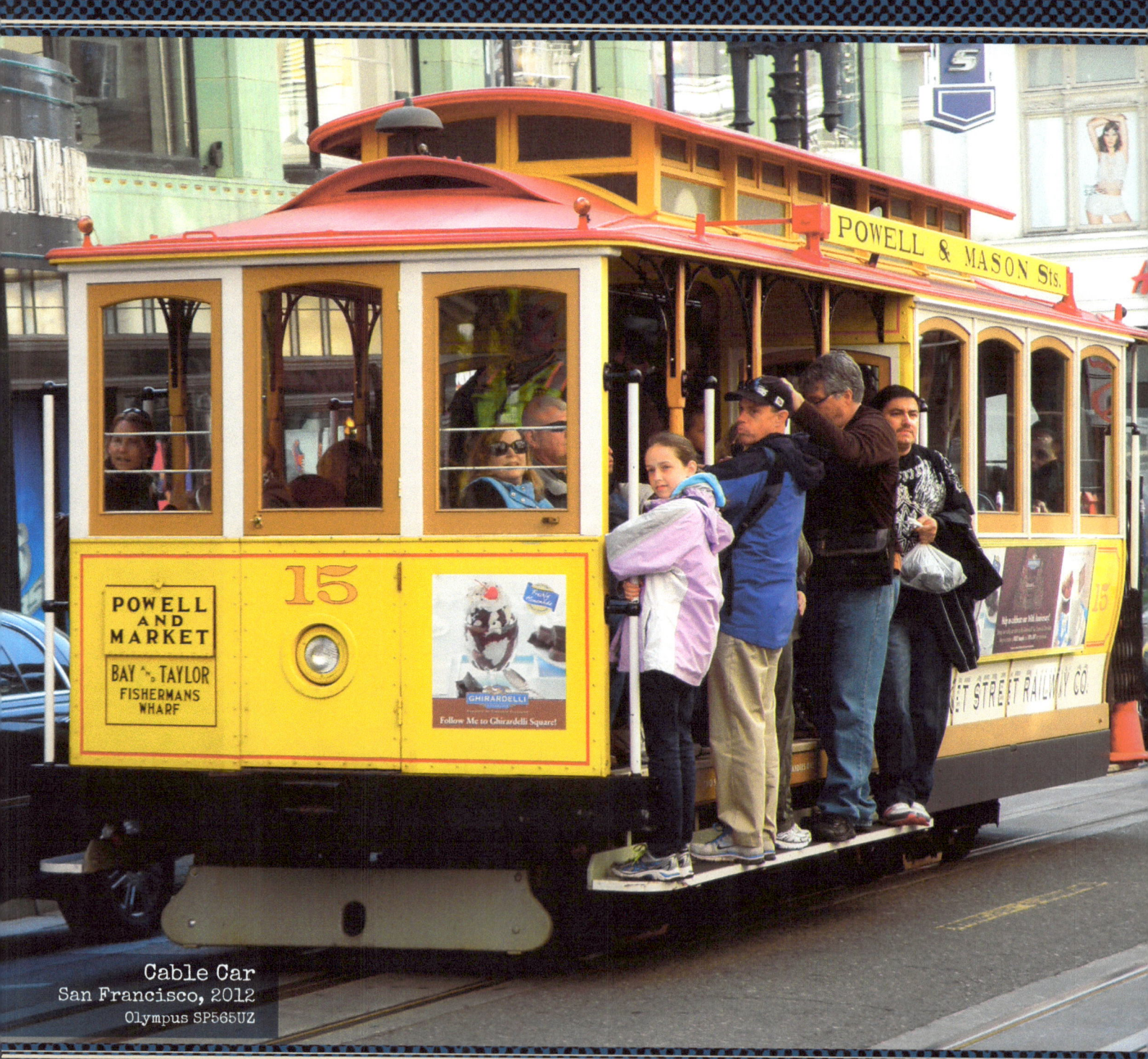

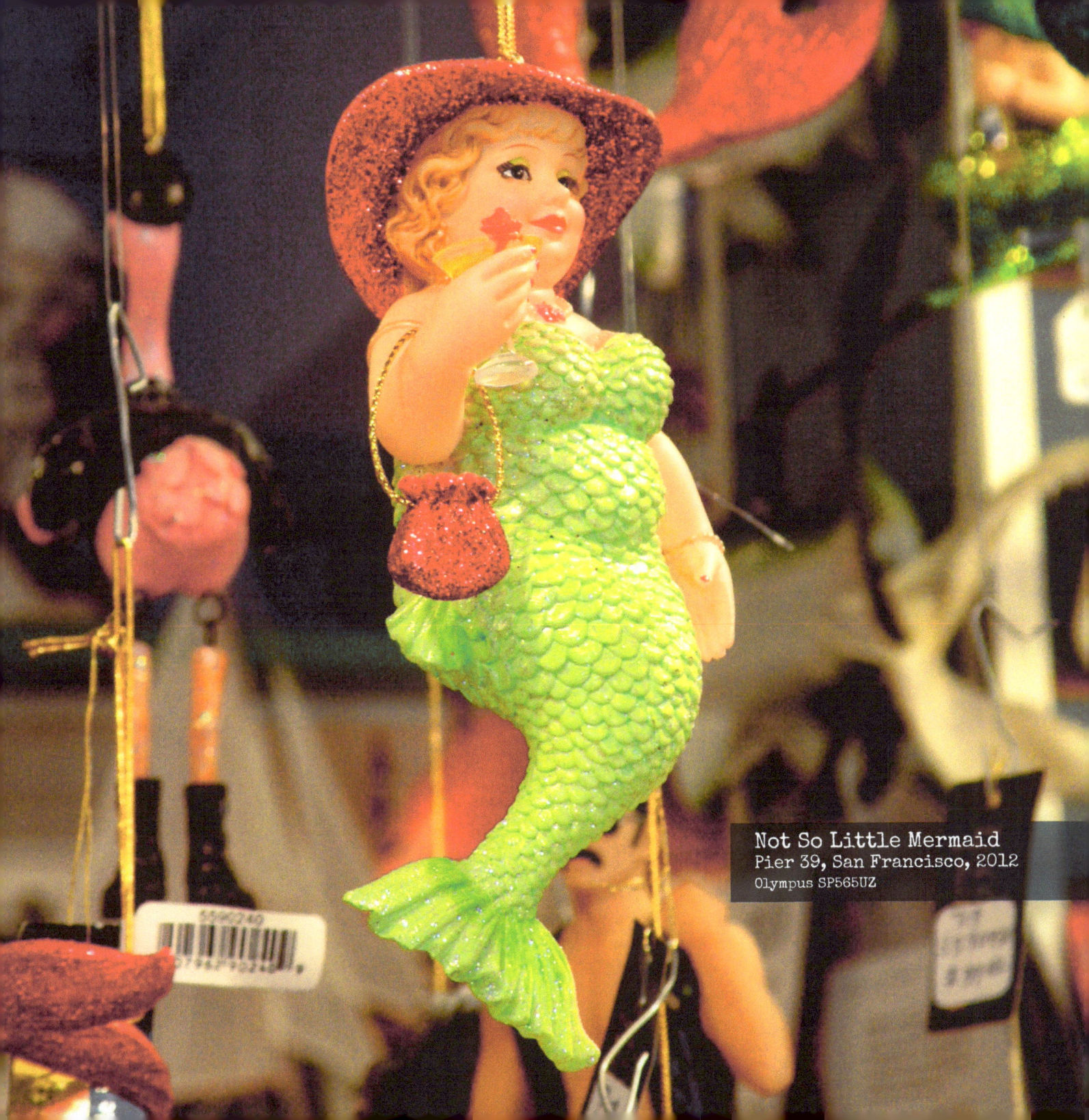

Not So Little Mermaid
Pier 39, San Francisco, 2012
Olympus SP565UZ

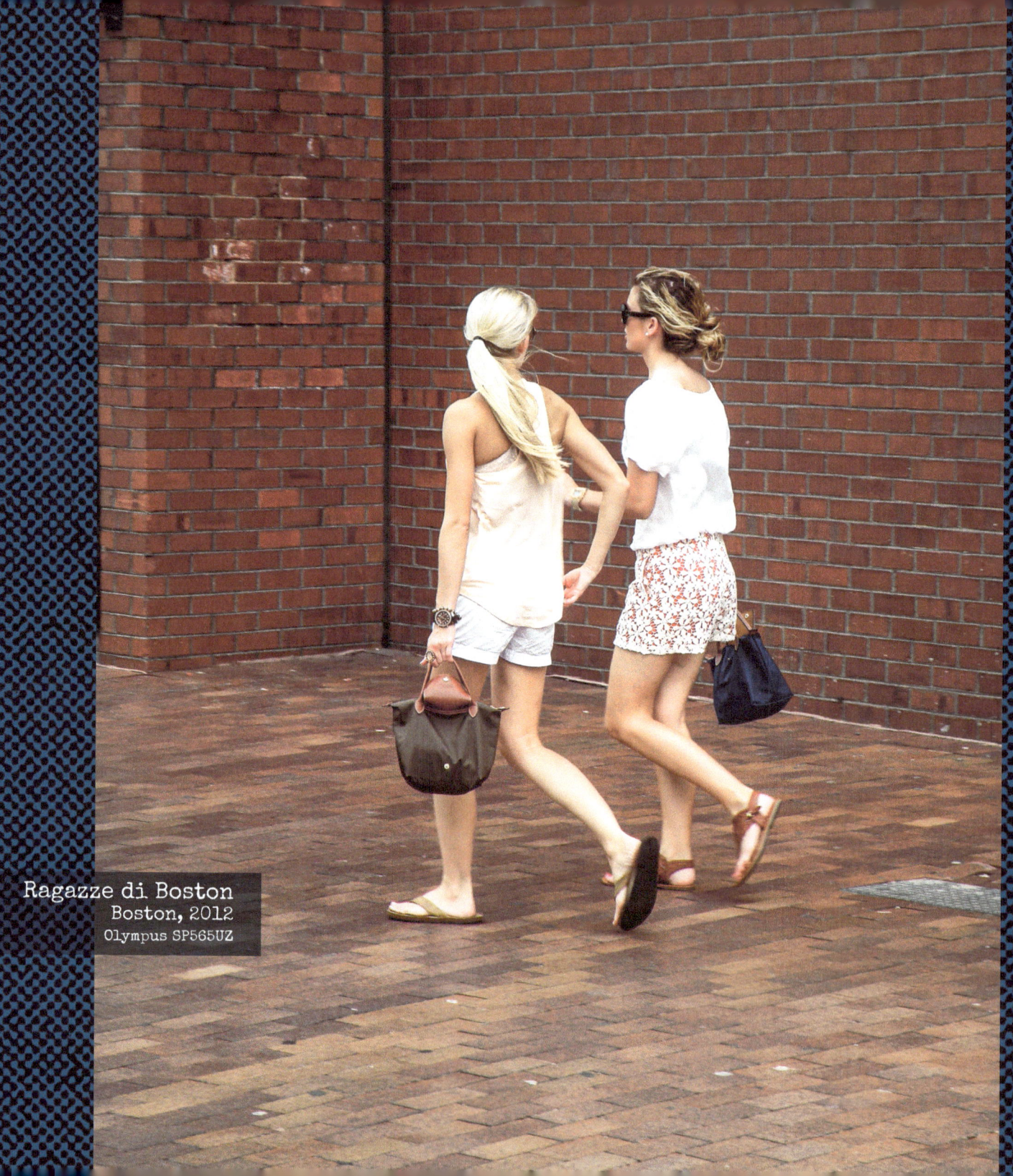

Ragazze di Boston
Boston, 2012
Olympus SP565UZ

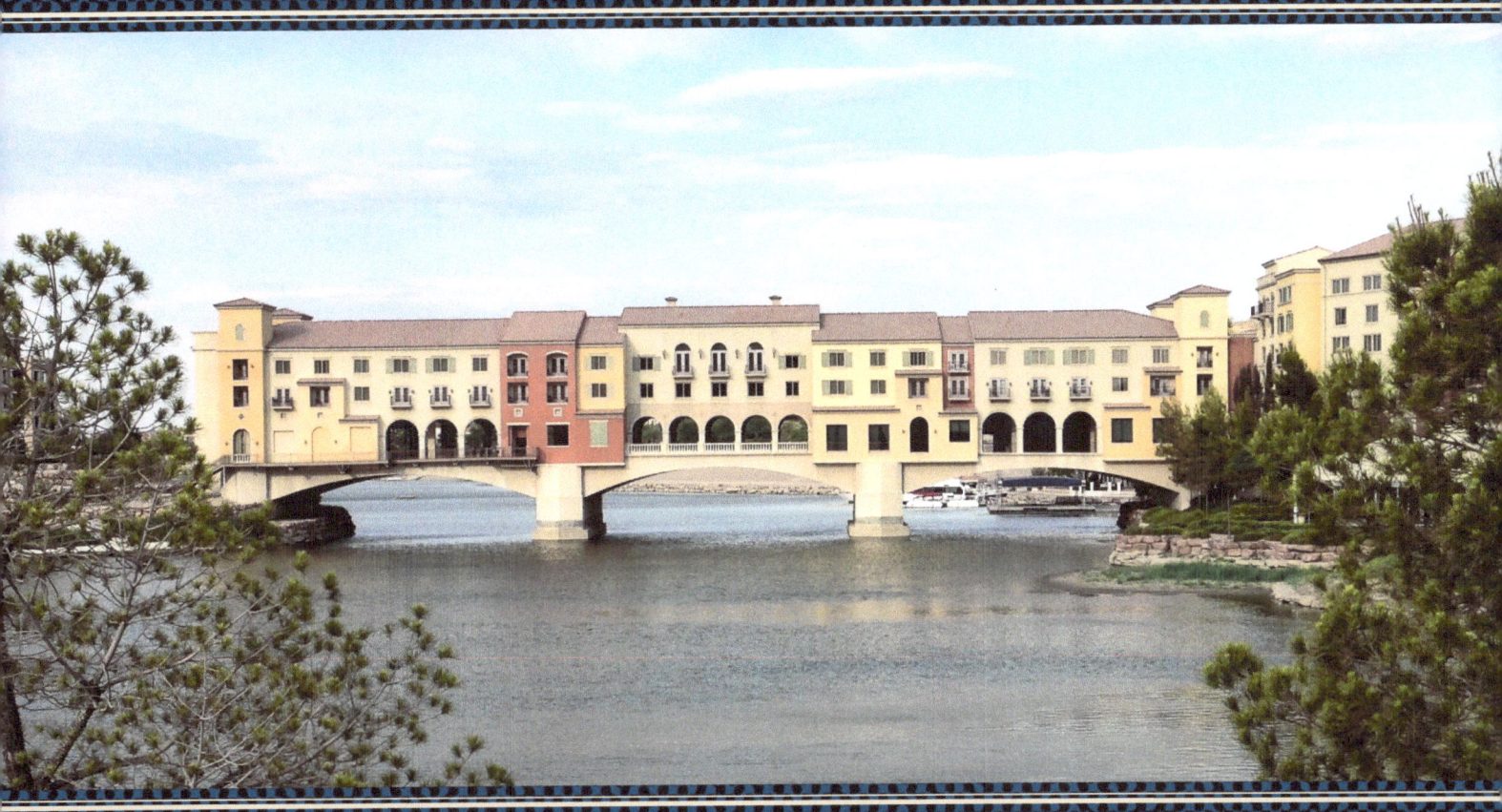

Hilton Ponte Vecchio
Lake Las Vegas, 2013
Apple iPhone 5

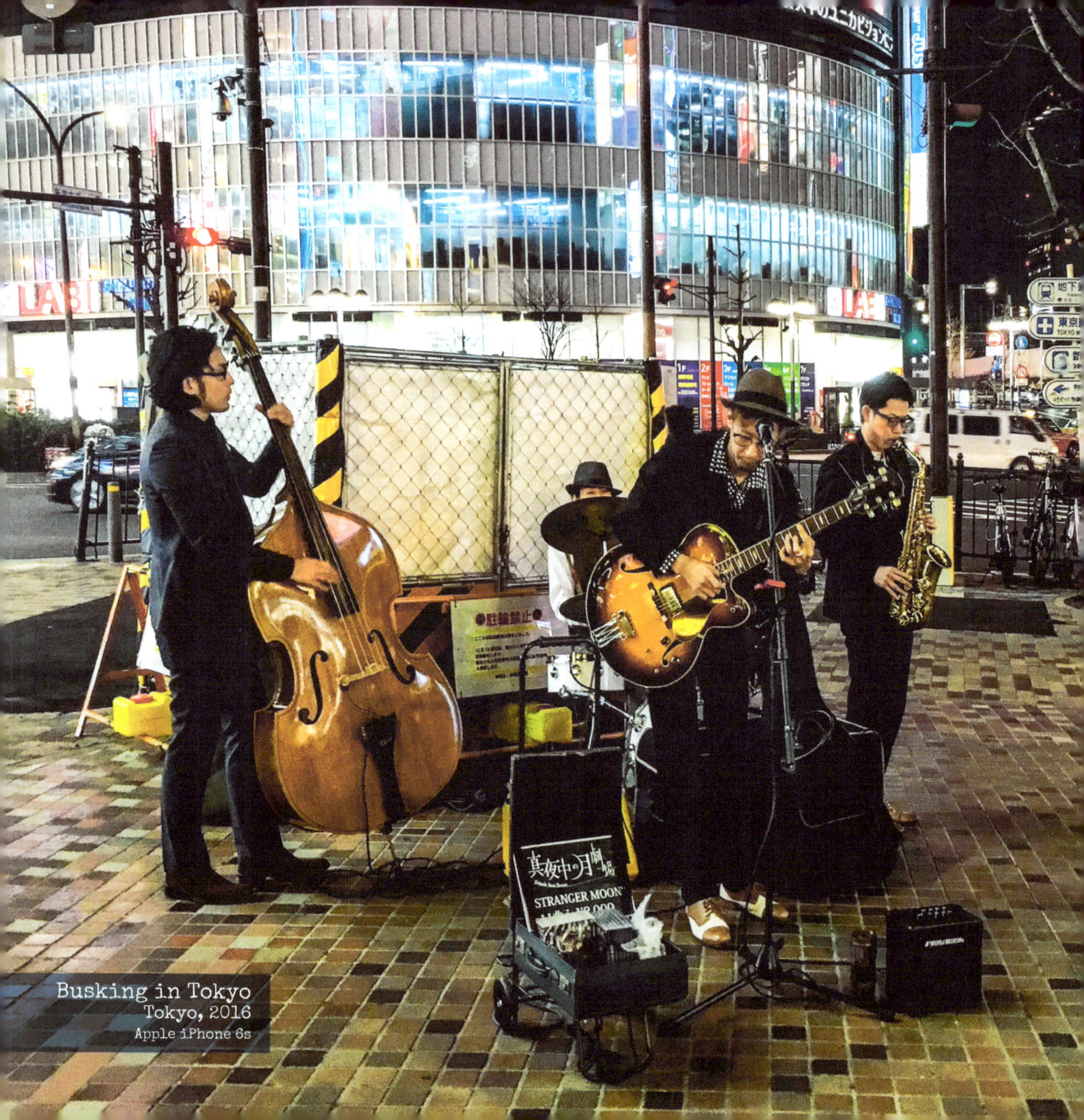

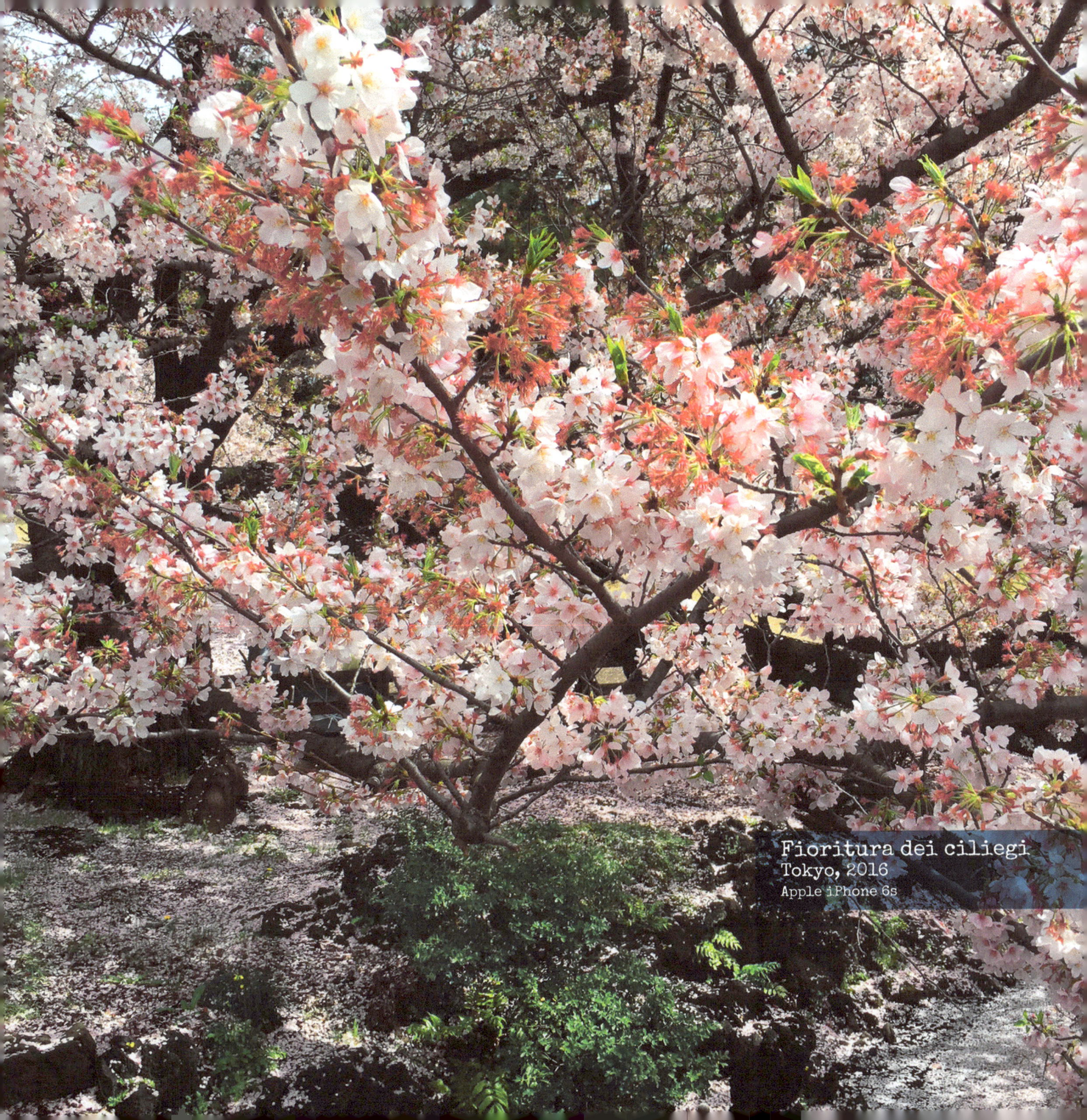

Fioritura dei ciliegi
Tokyo, 2016
Apple iPhone 6s

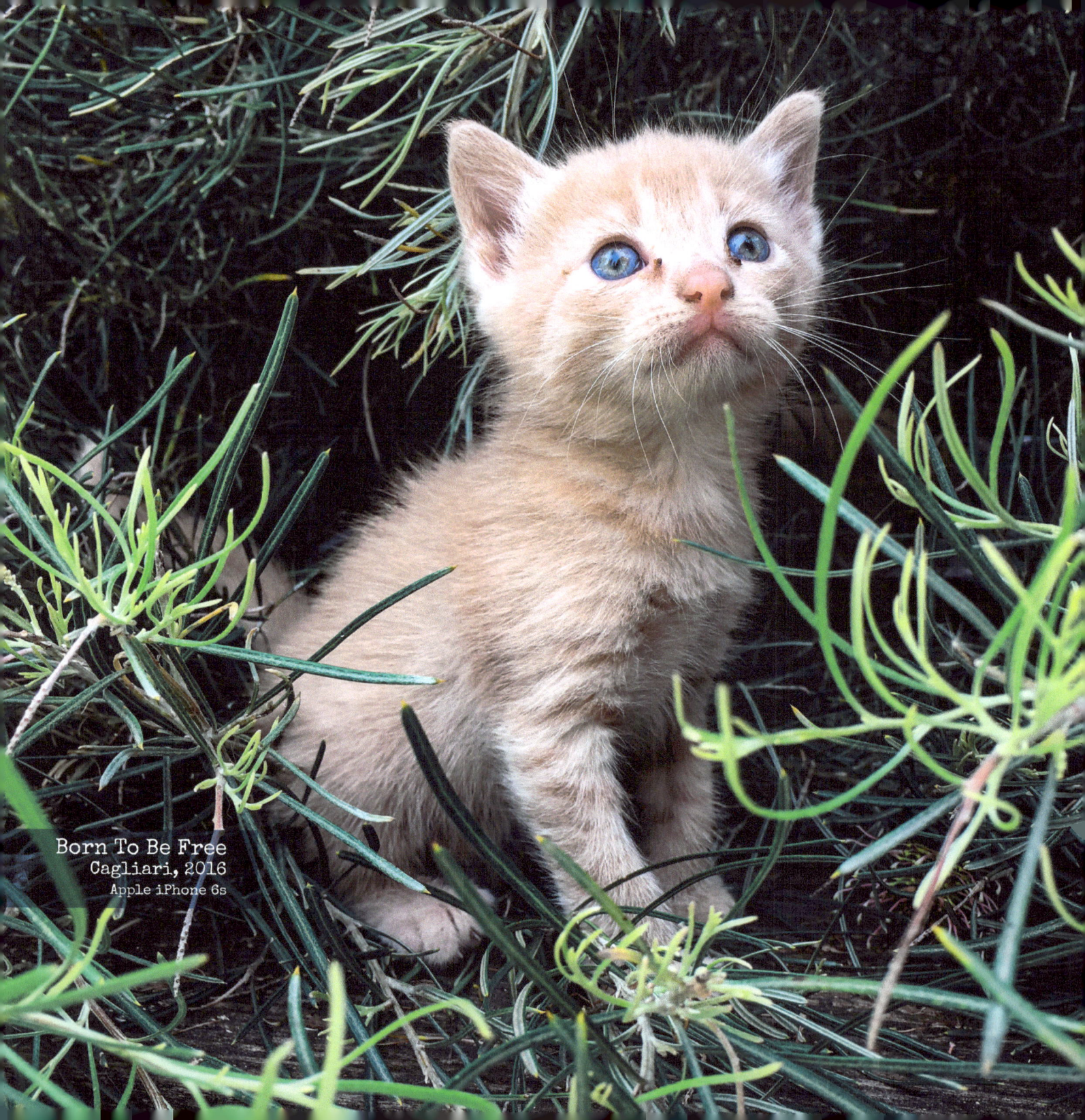

Born To Be Free
Cagliari, 2016
Apple iPhone 6s

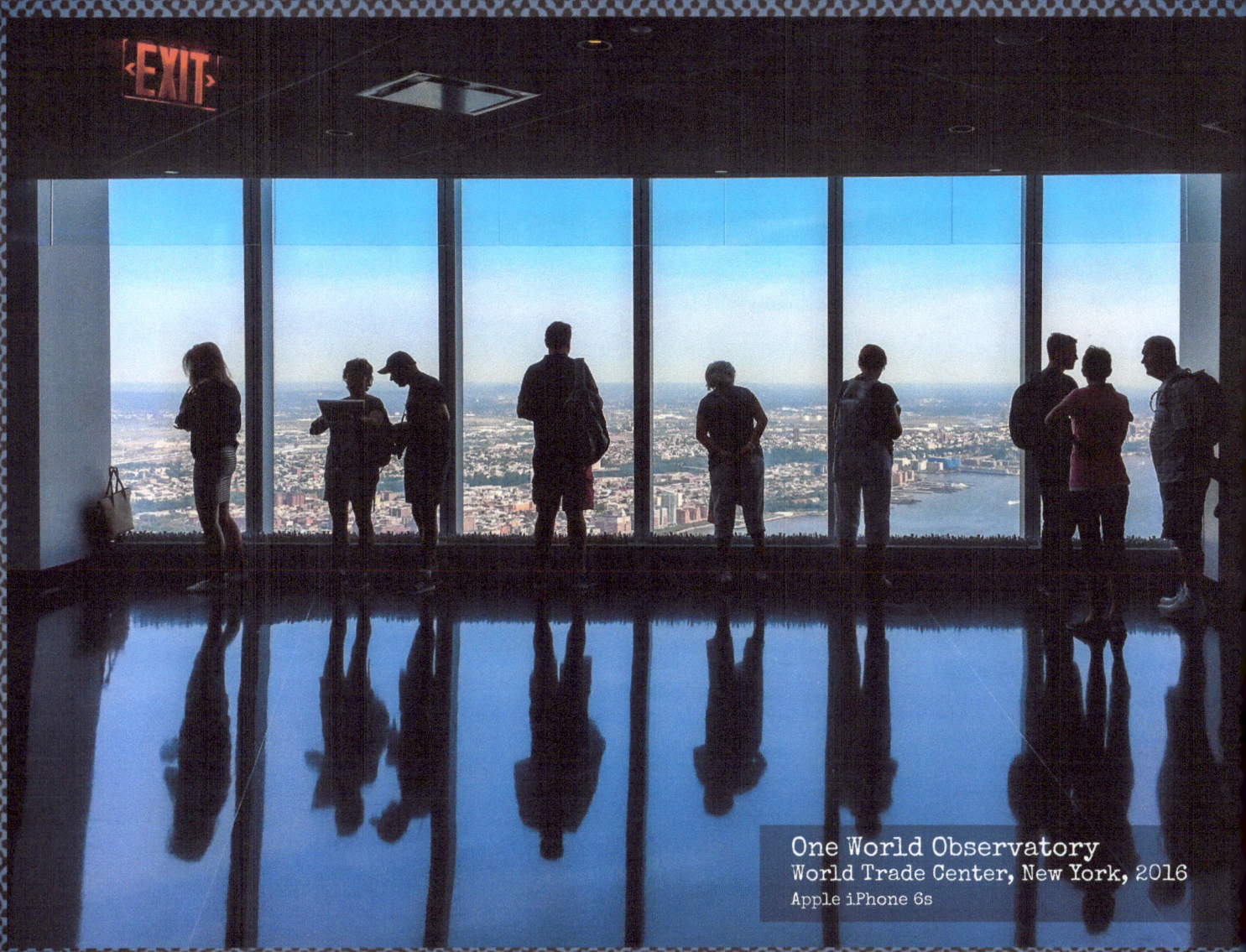

One World Observatory
World Trade Center, New York, 2016
Apple iPhone 6s

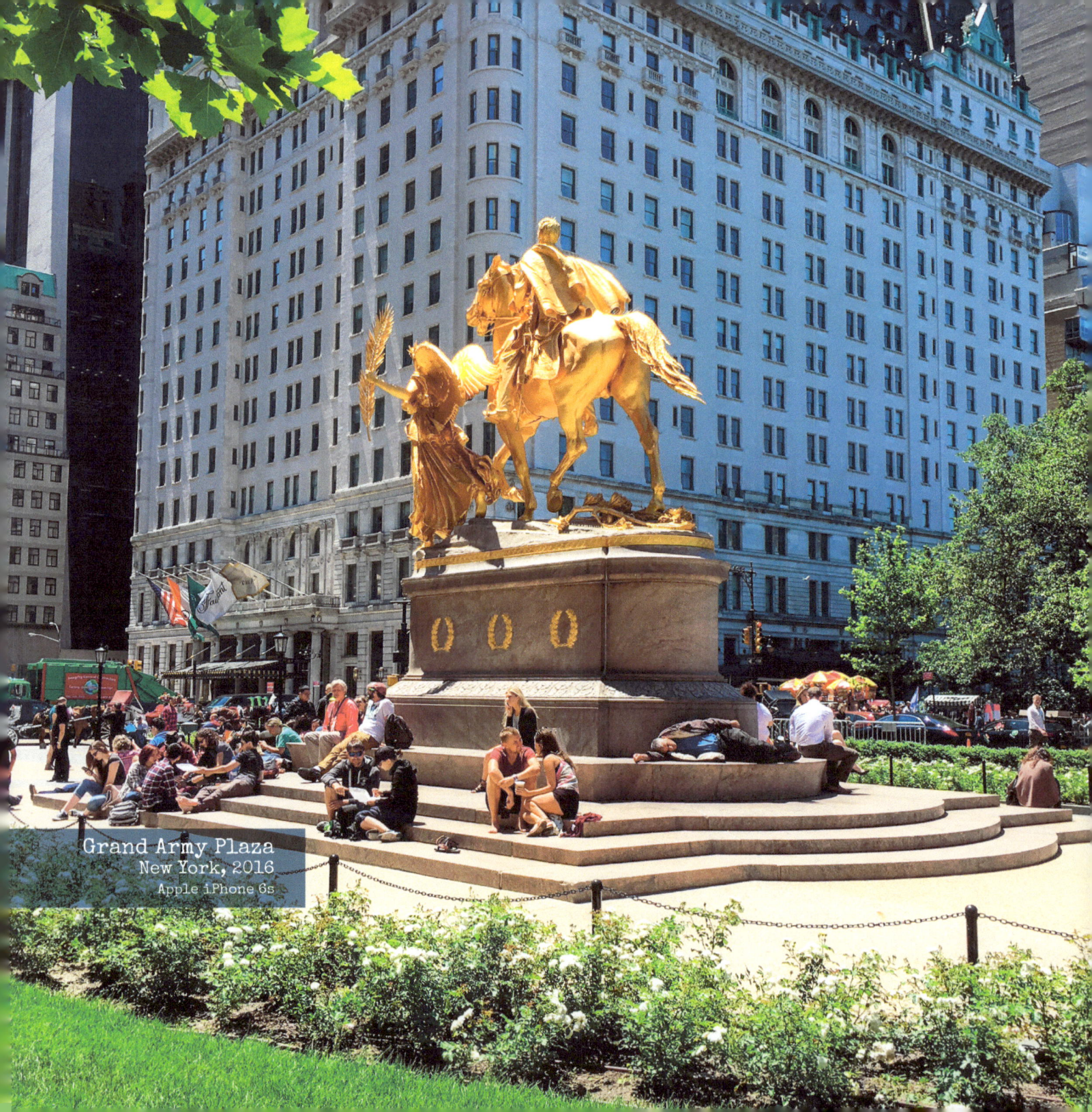

Grand Army Plaza
New York, 2016
Apple iPhone 6s

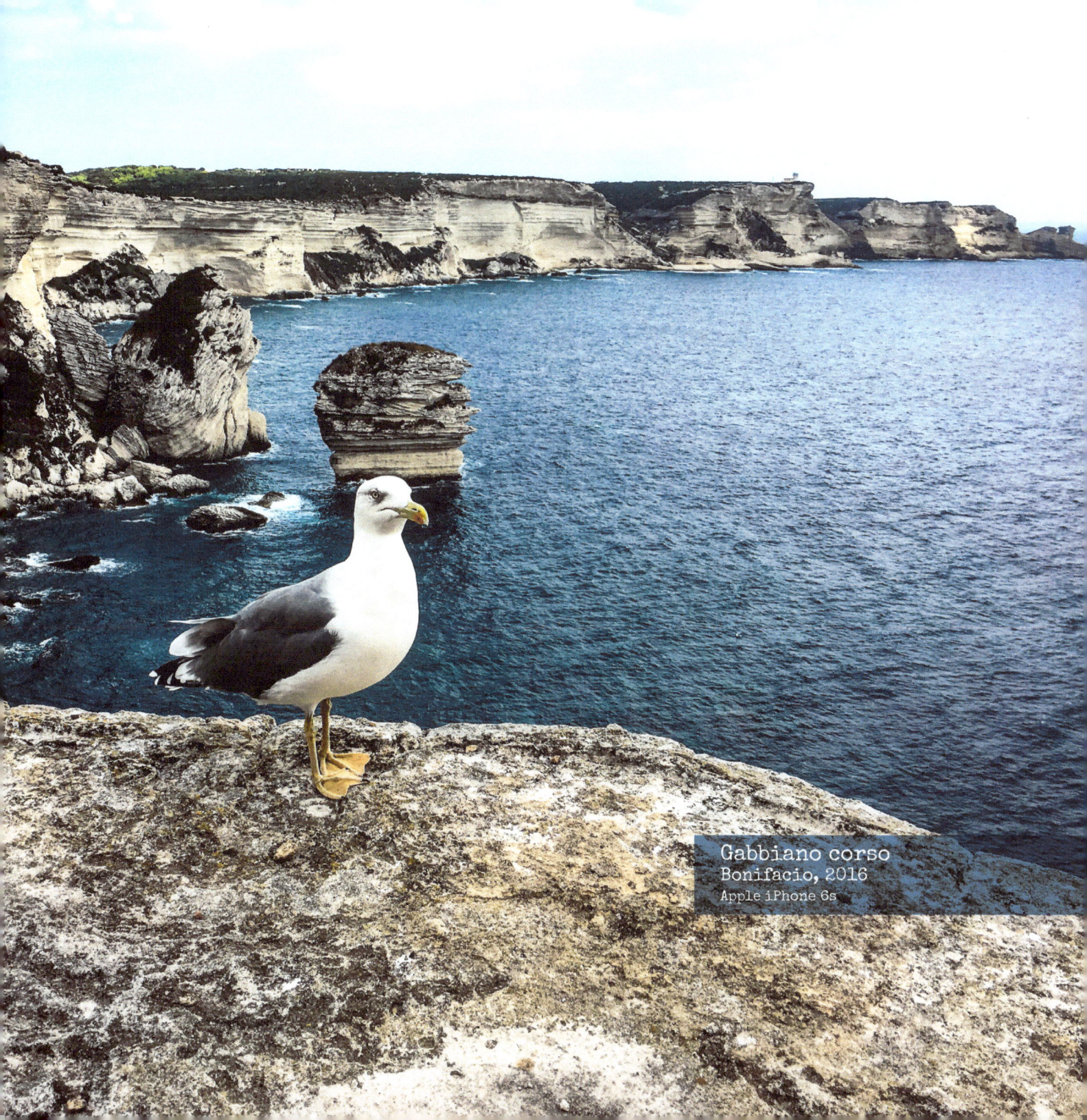

Gabbiano corso
Bonifacio, 2016
Apple iPhone 6s

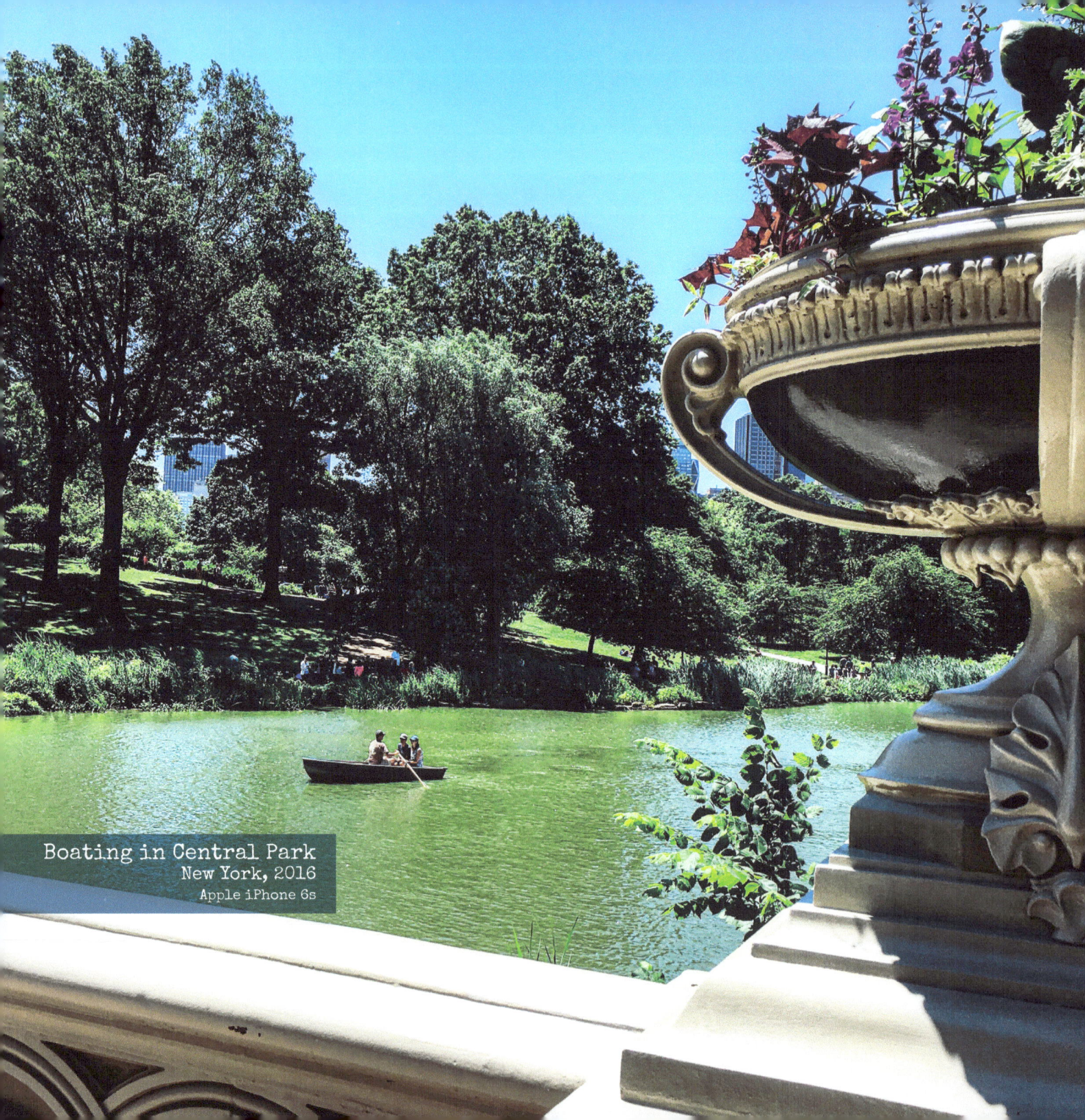

Boating in Central Park
New York, 2016
Apple iPhone 6s

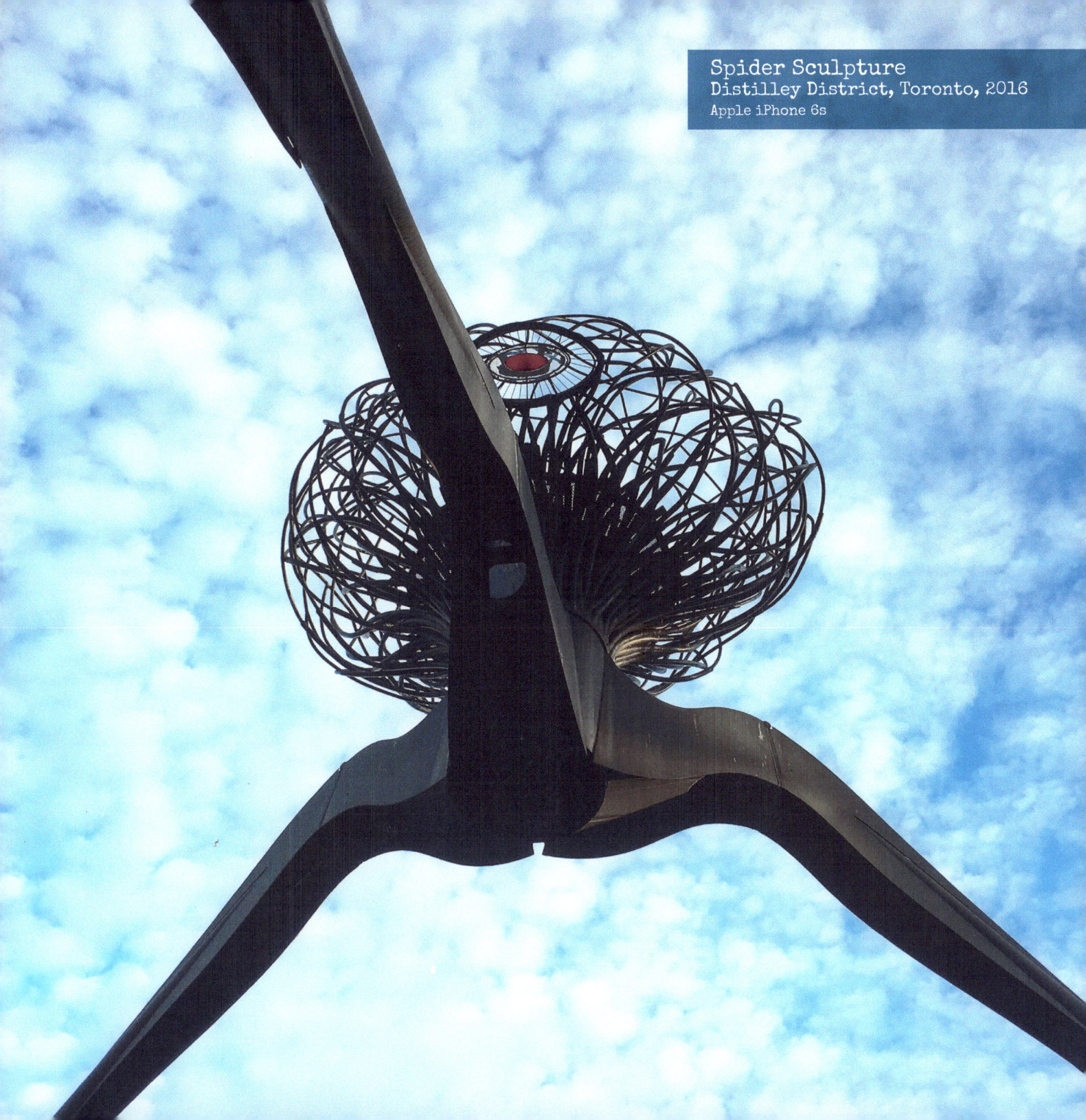

Spider Sculpture
Distilley District, Toronto, 2016
Apple iPhone 6s

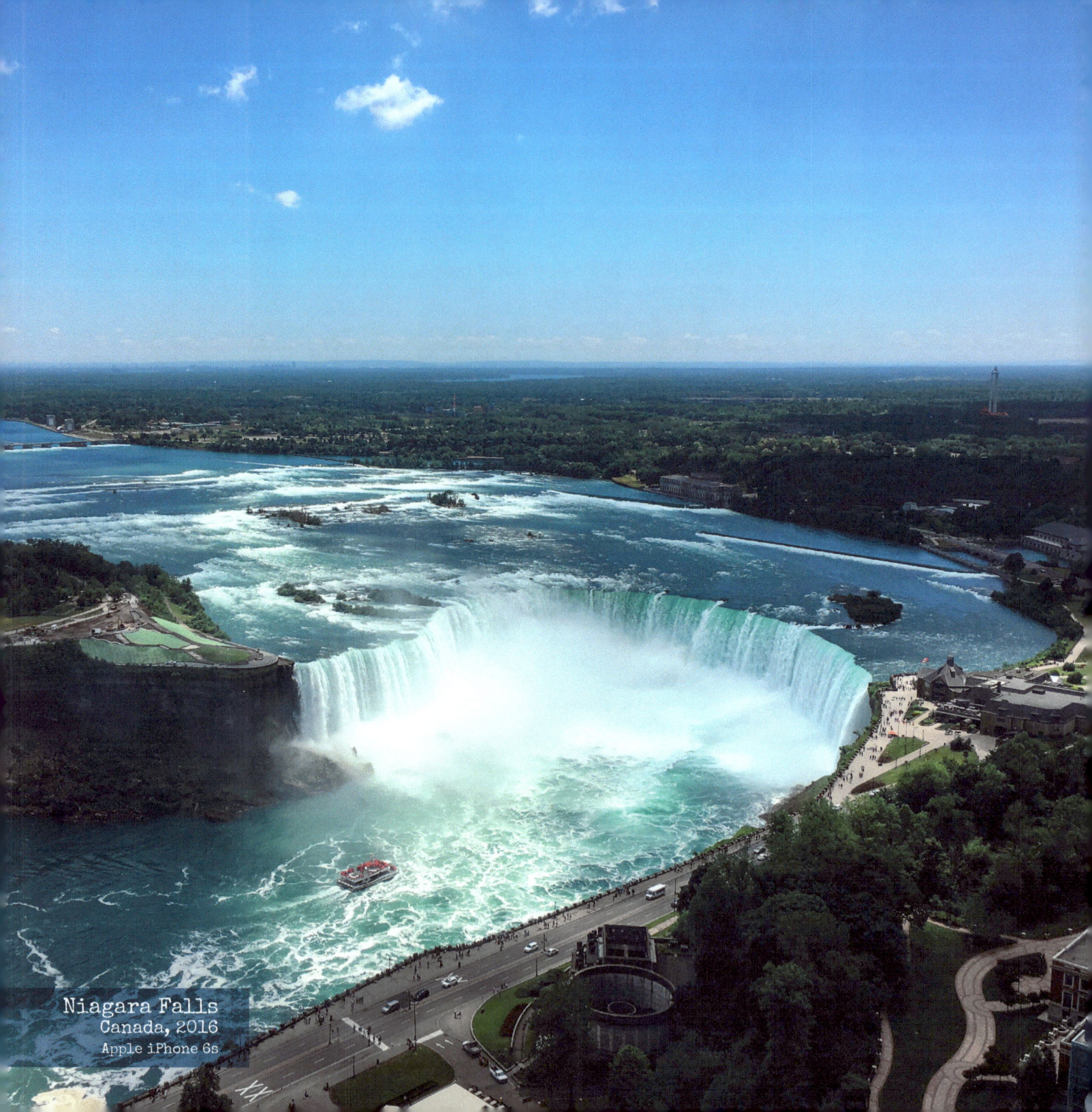

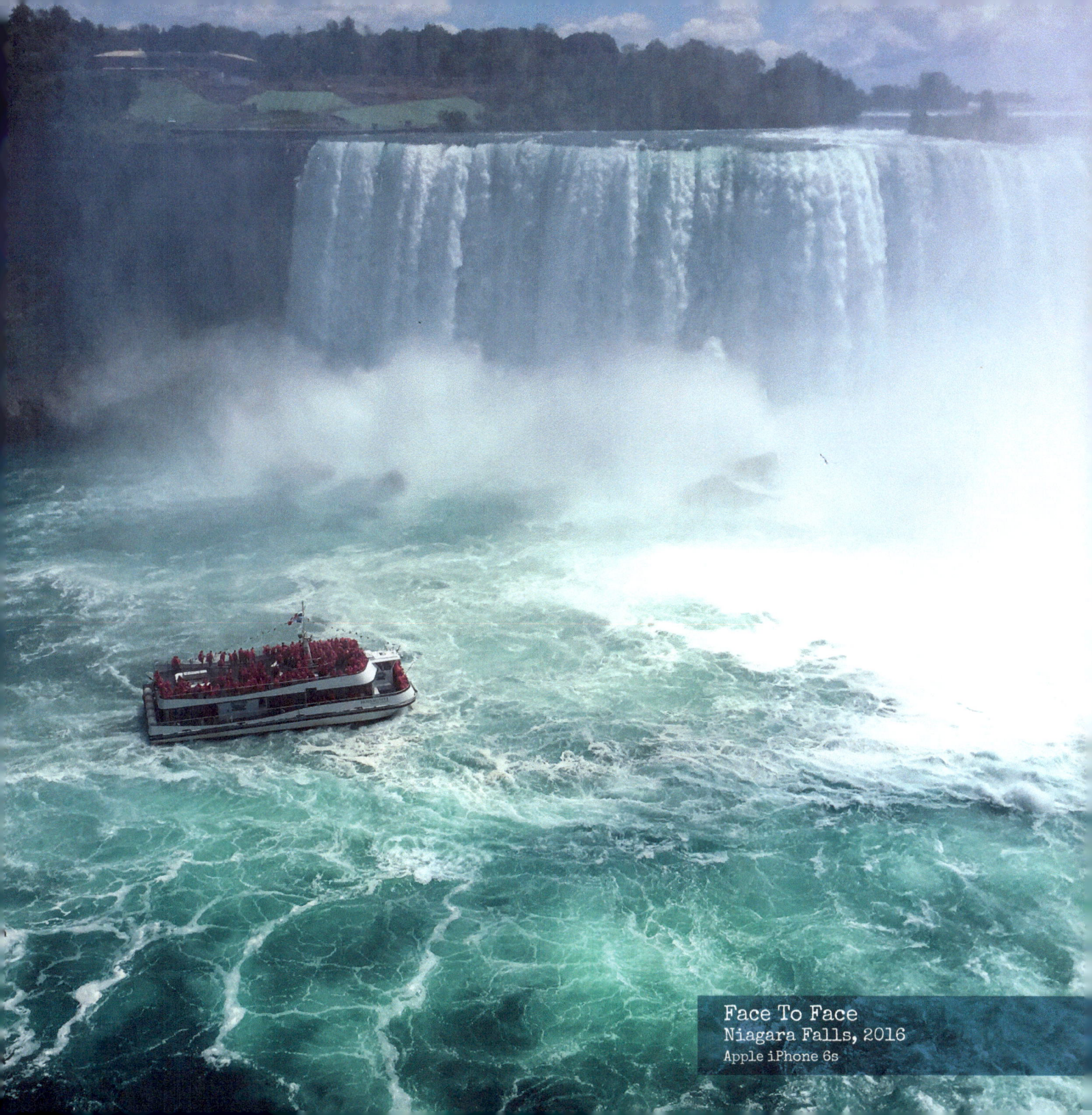

Face To Face
Niagara Falls, 2016
Apple iPhone 6s

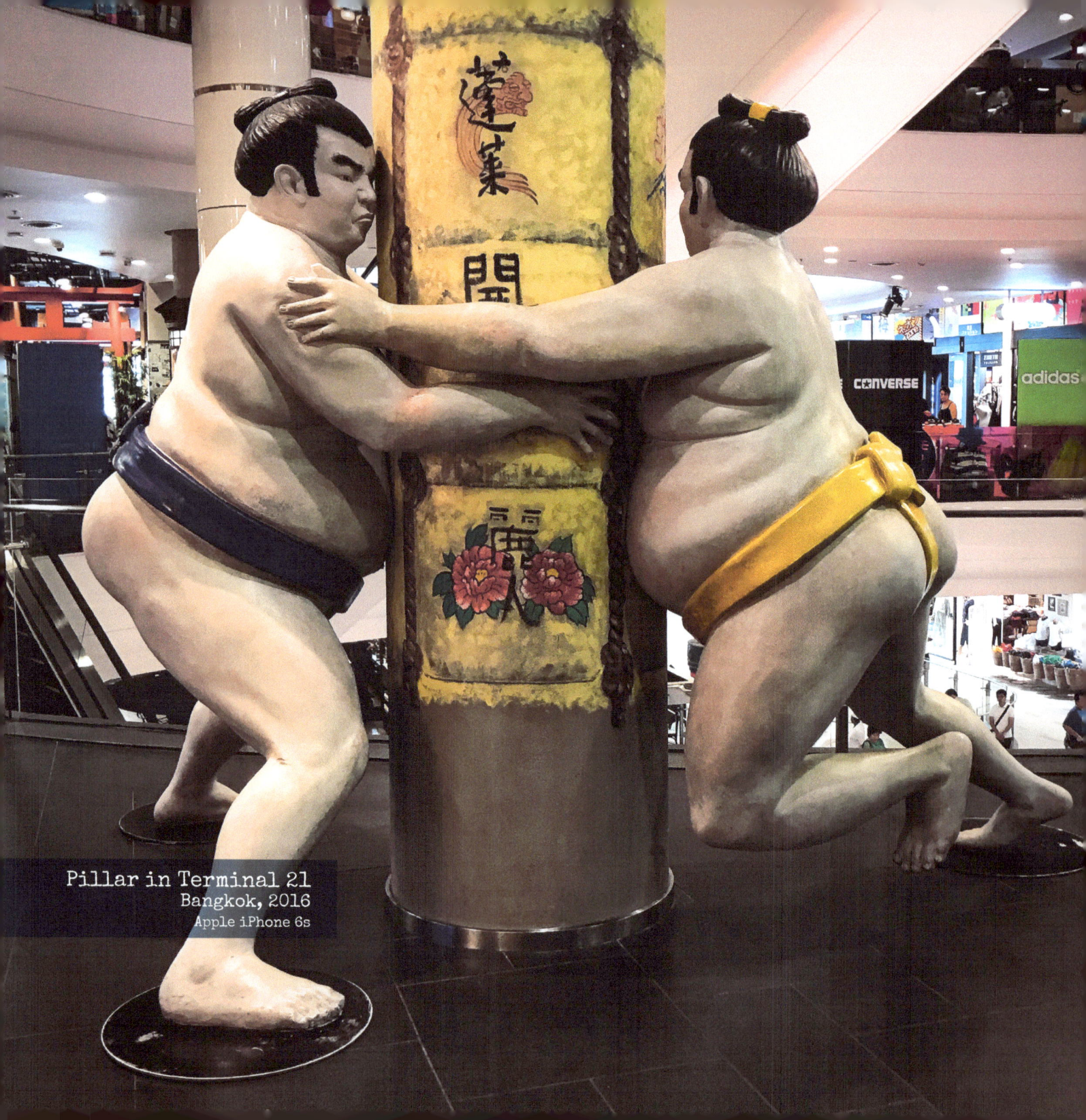

Pillar in Terminal 21
Bangkok, 2016
Apple iPhone 6s

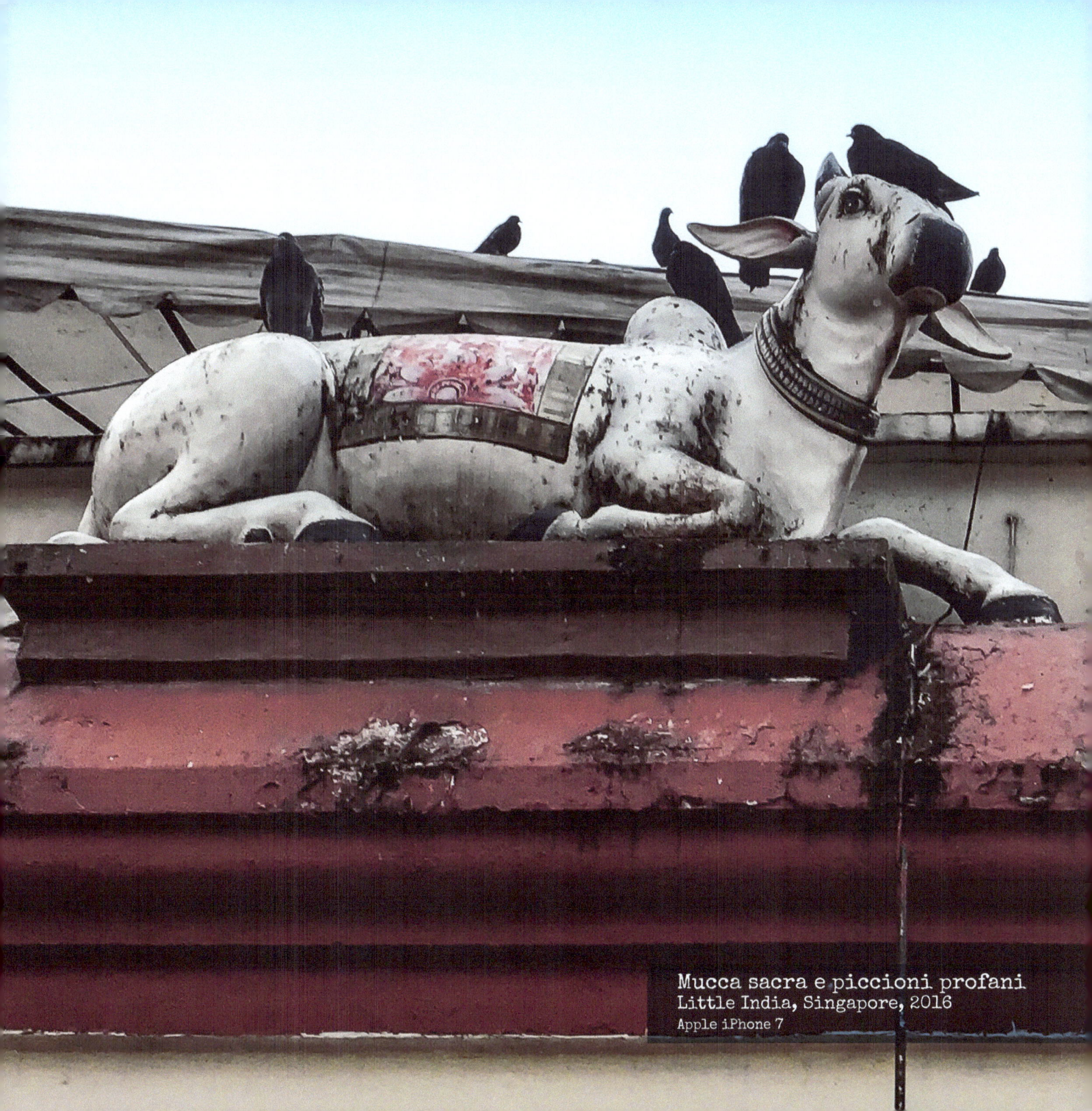

Mucca sacra e piccioni profani
Little India, Singapore, 2016
Apple iPhone 7

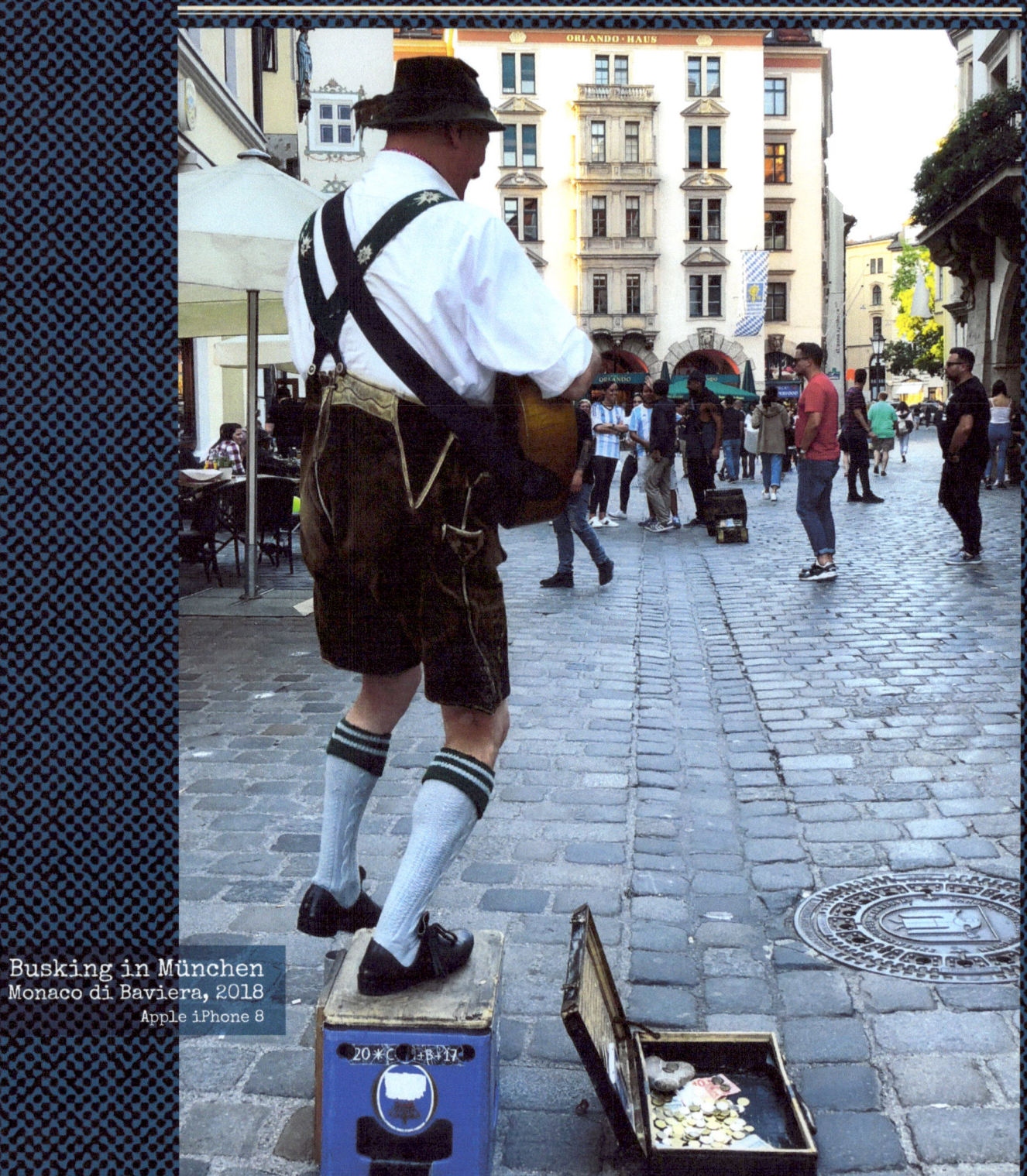

Busking in München
Monaco di Baviera, 2018
Apple iPhone 8

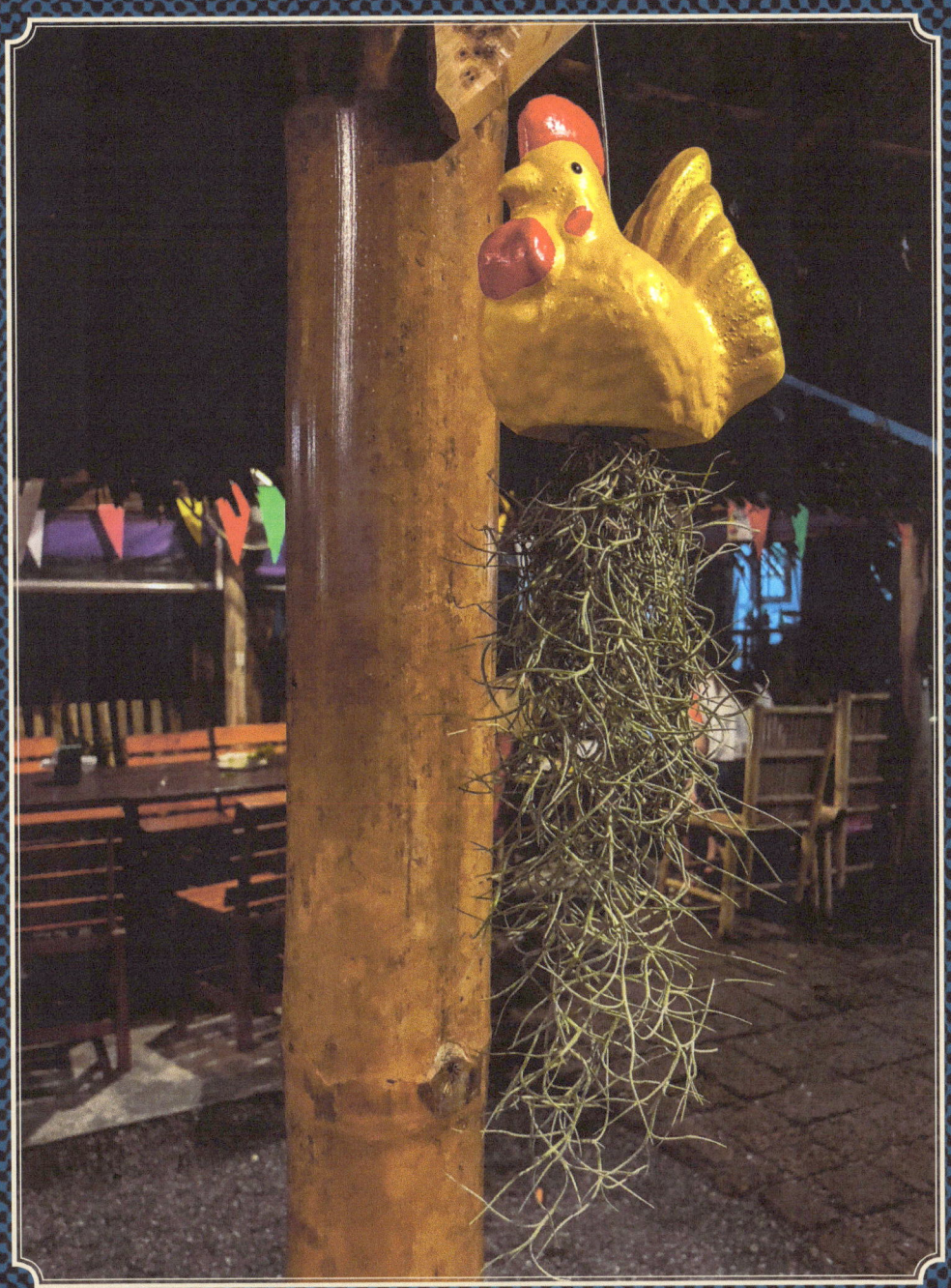

Restaurant in Phuket Laguna
Thailand, 2017
Apple iPhone 8

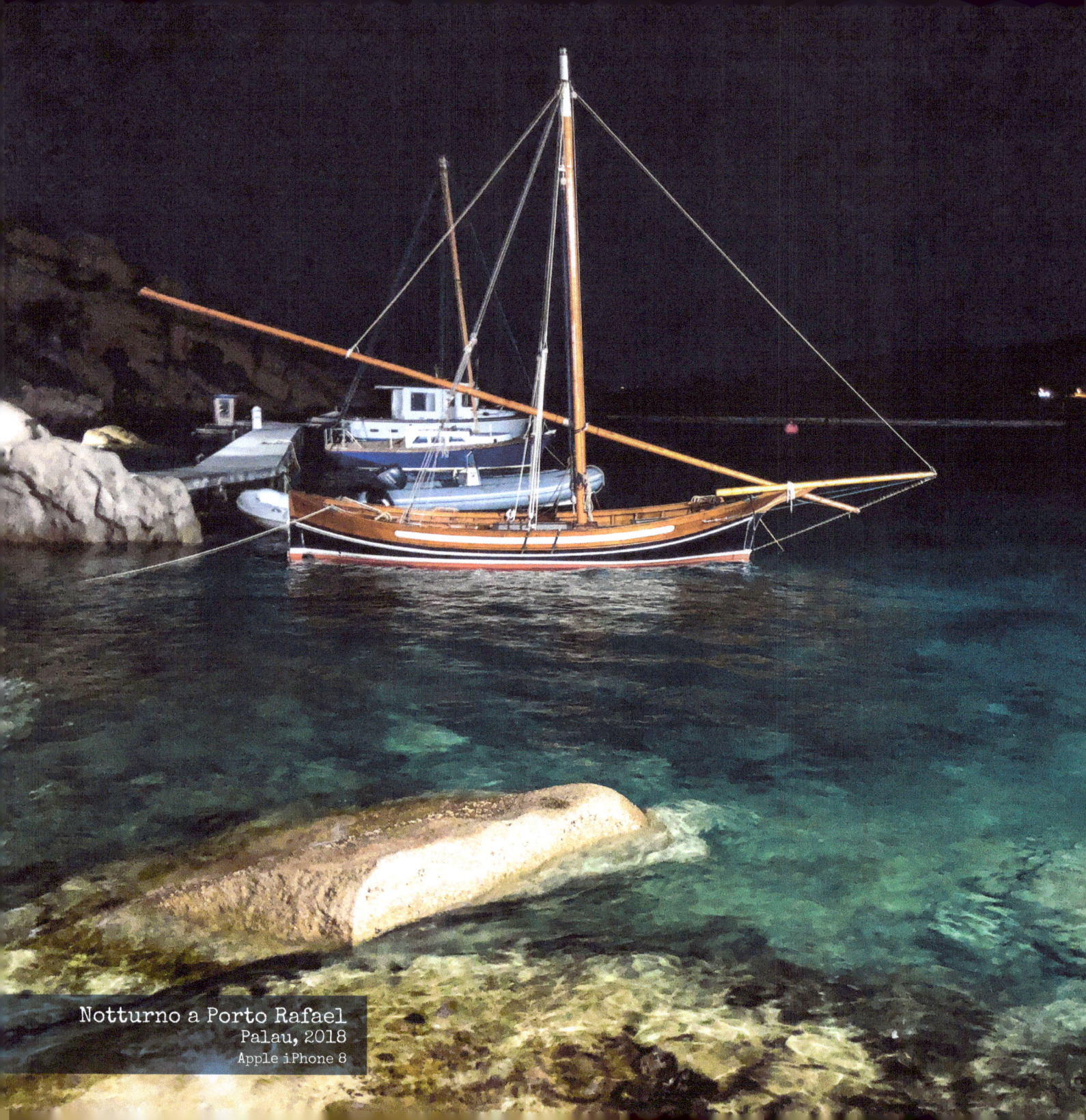

Notturno a Porto Rafael
Palau, 2018
Apple iPhone 8

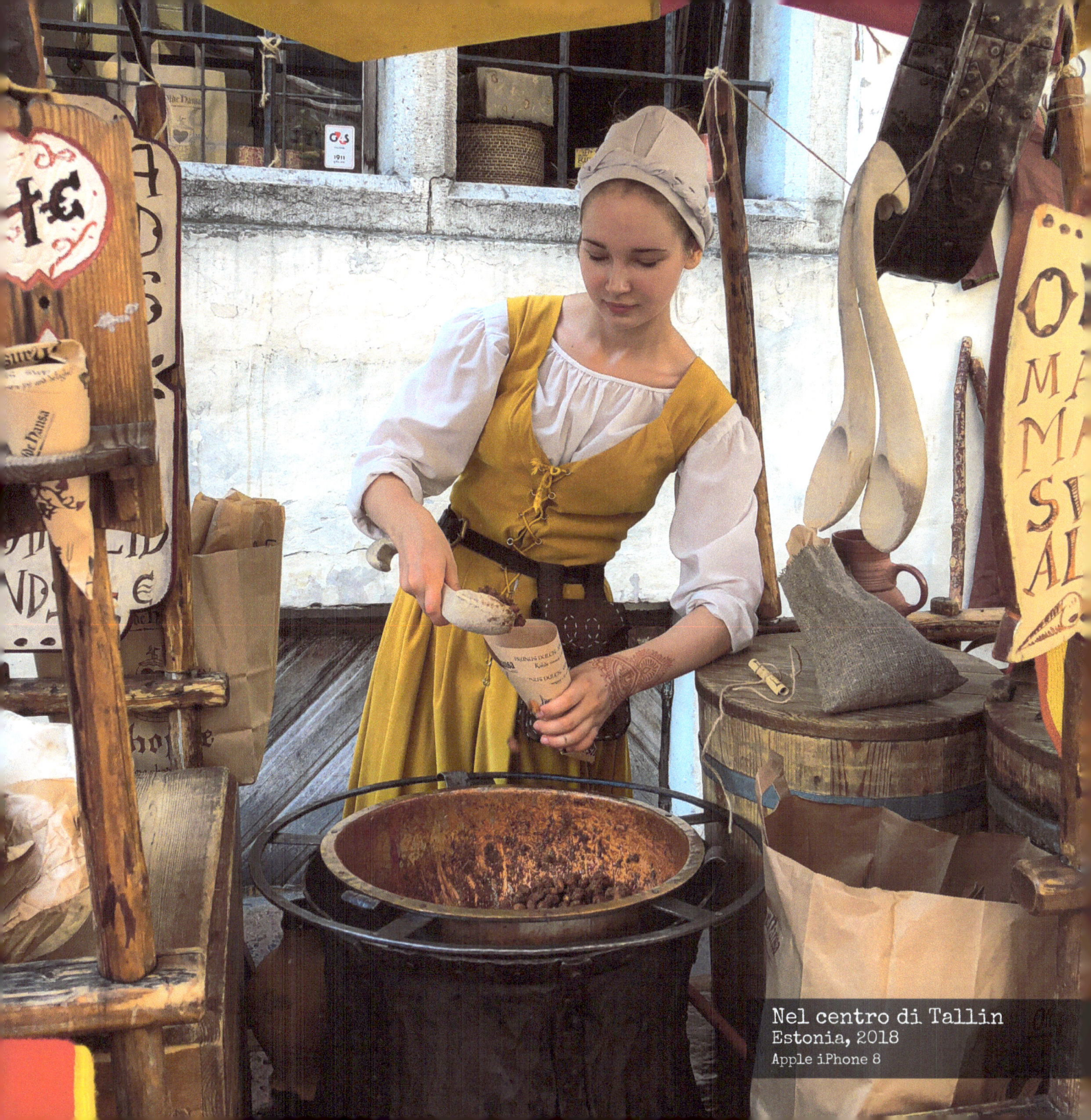

Nel centro di Tallin
Estonia, 2018
Apple iPhone 8

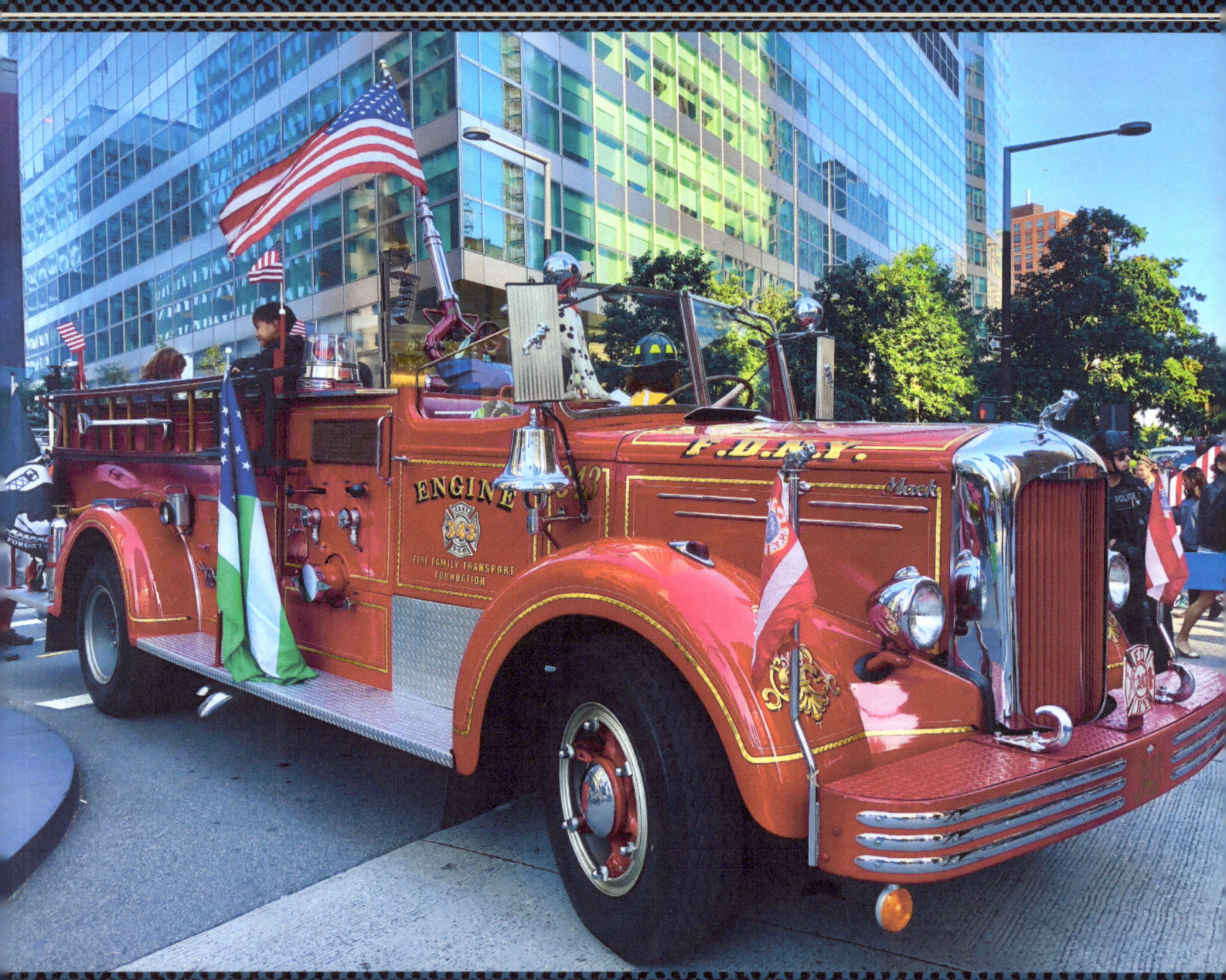

Auto storica N.Y. Fire Department
New York, 2018
Apple iPhone 8

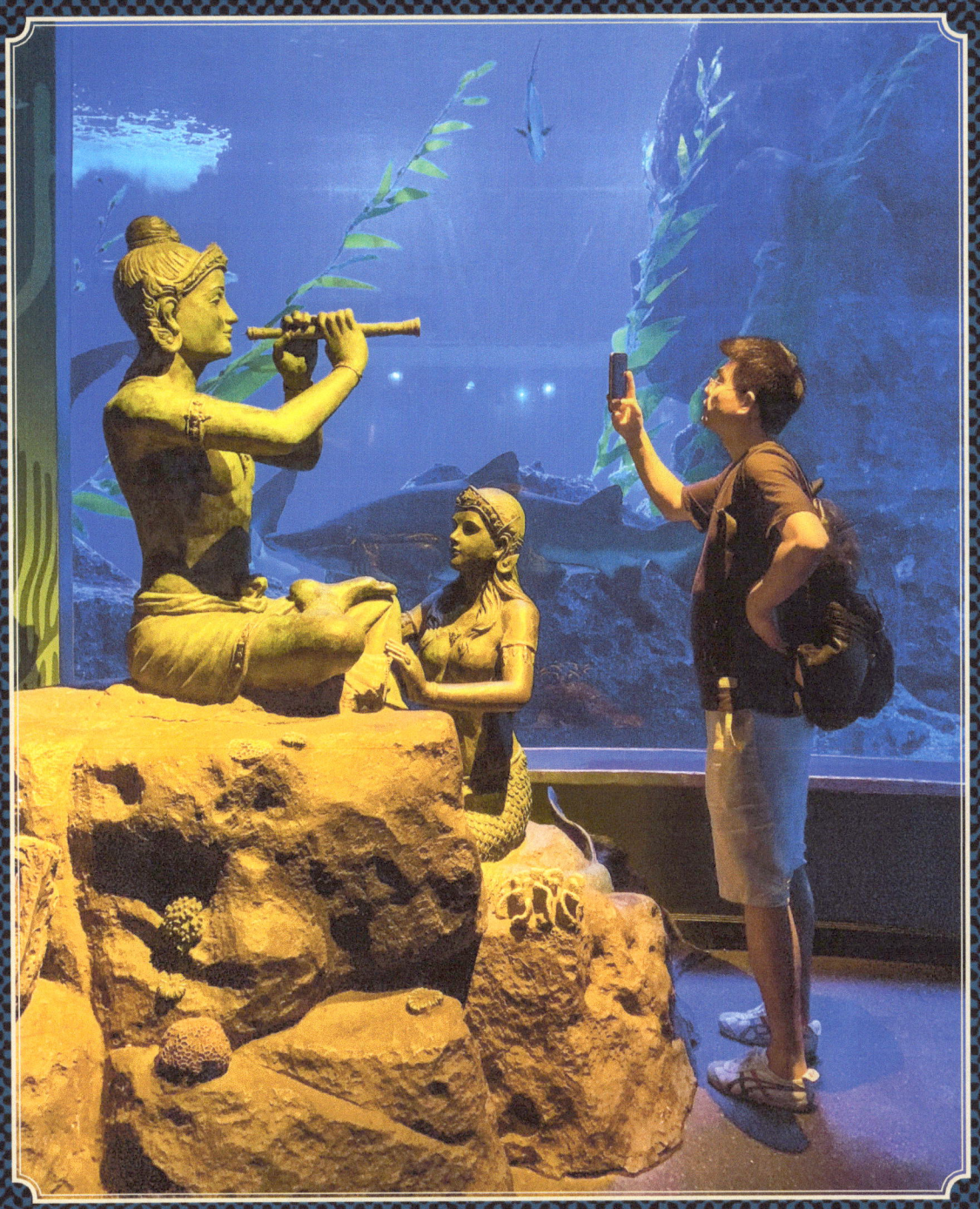

Sea Life World Aquarium
Bangkok, 2018
Apple iPhone XS

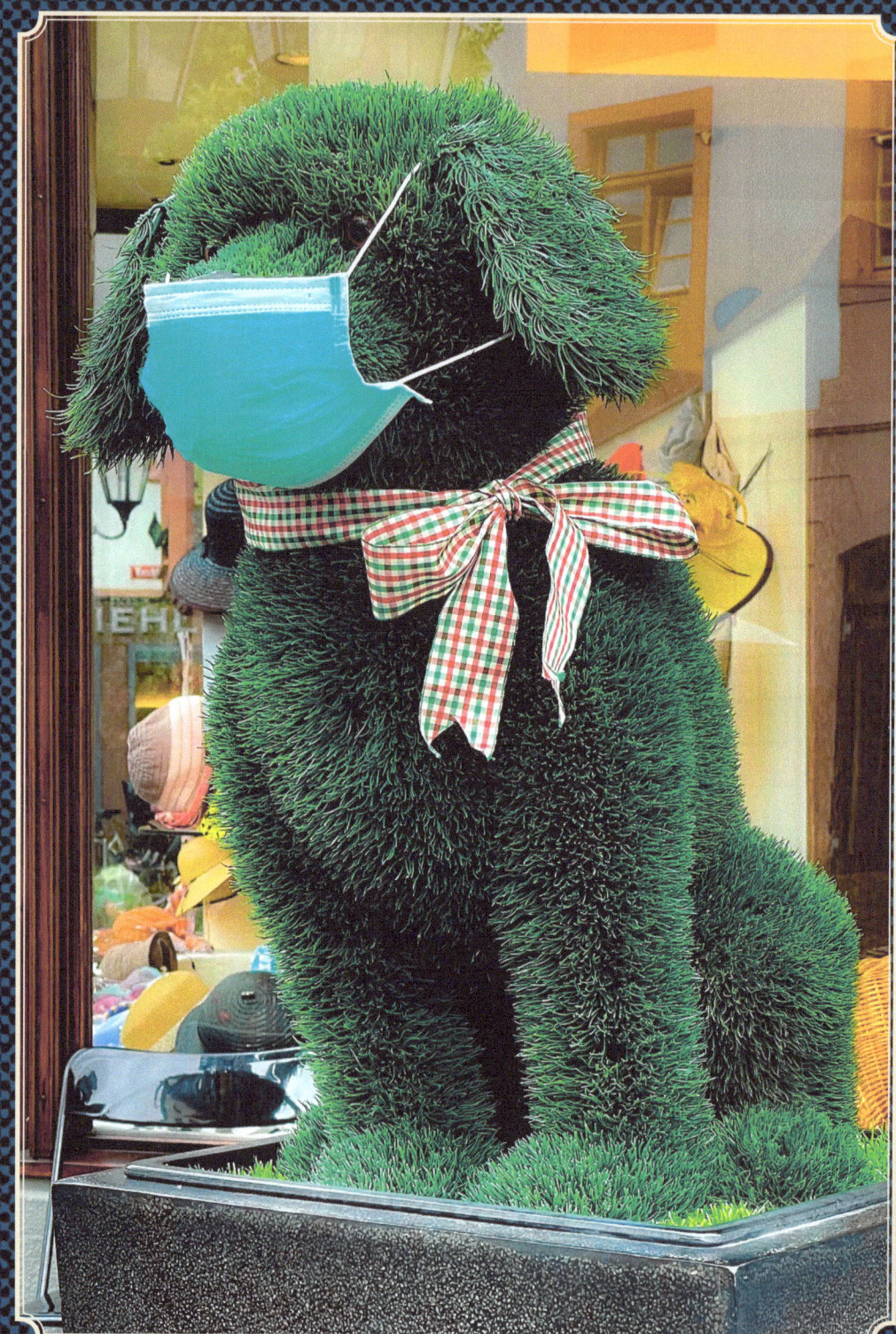

Pandemia
Mainz, 2021
Apple iPhone 12pro

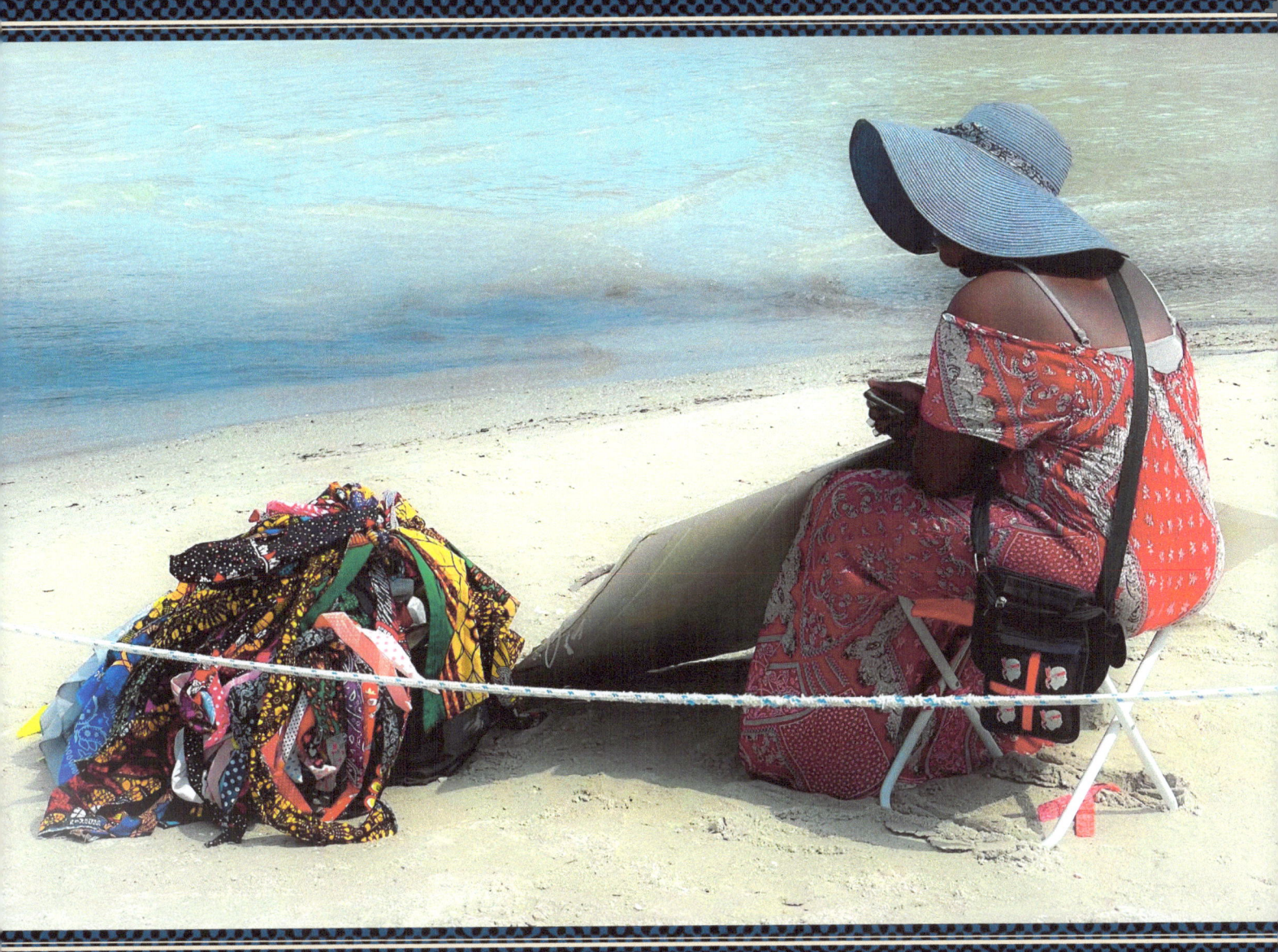

Fine stagione
Puntaldia, spiaggia l'Impostu, 2021
Apple iPhone 12pro

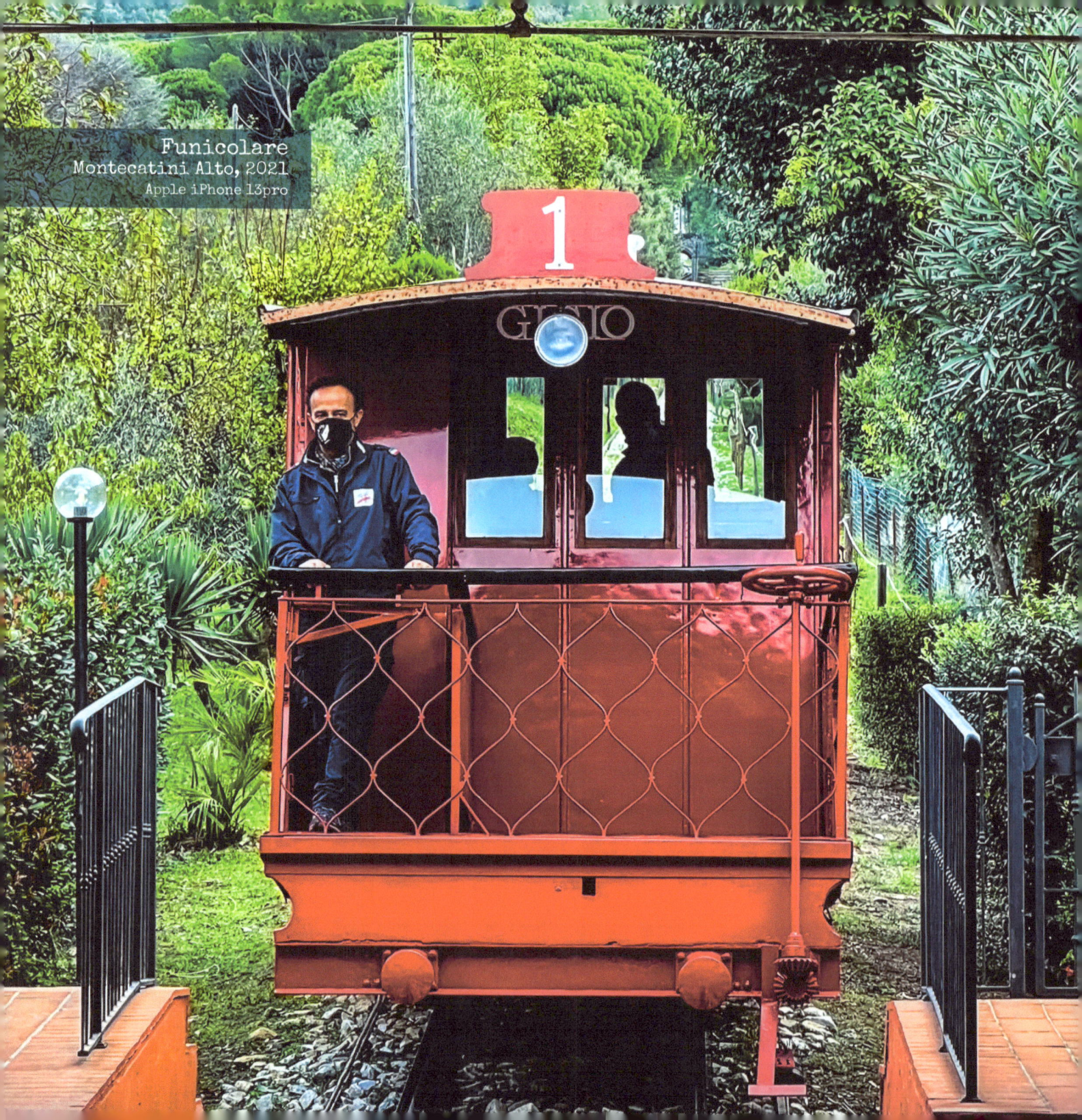

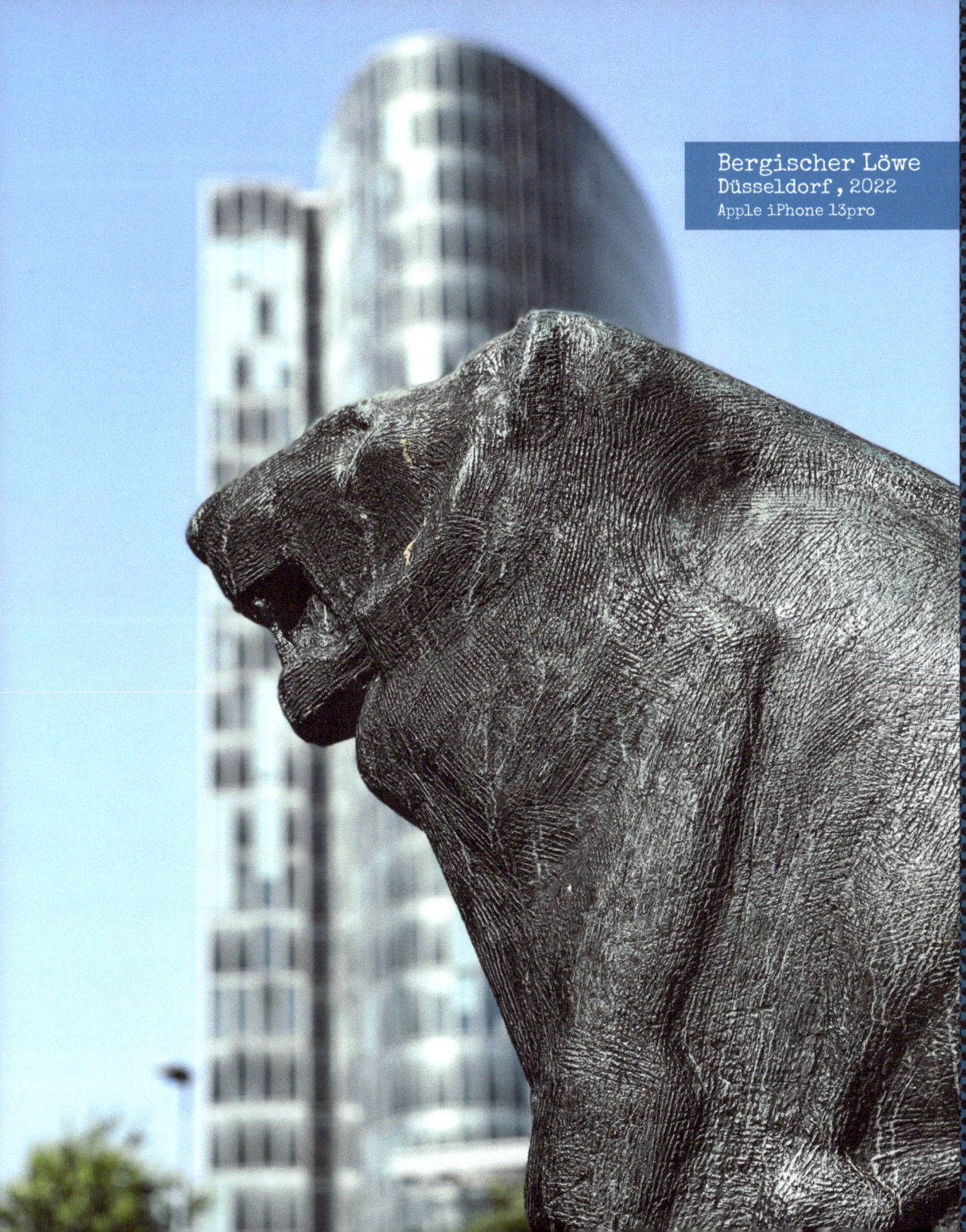

Bergischer Löwe
Düsseldorf, 2022
Apple iPhone 13pro

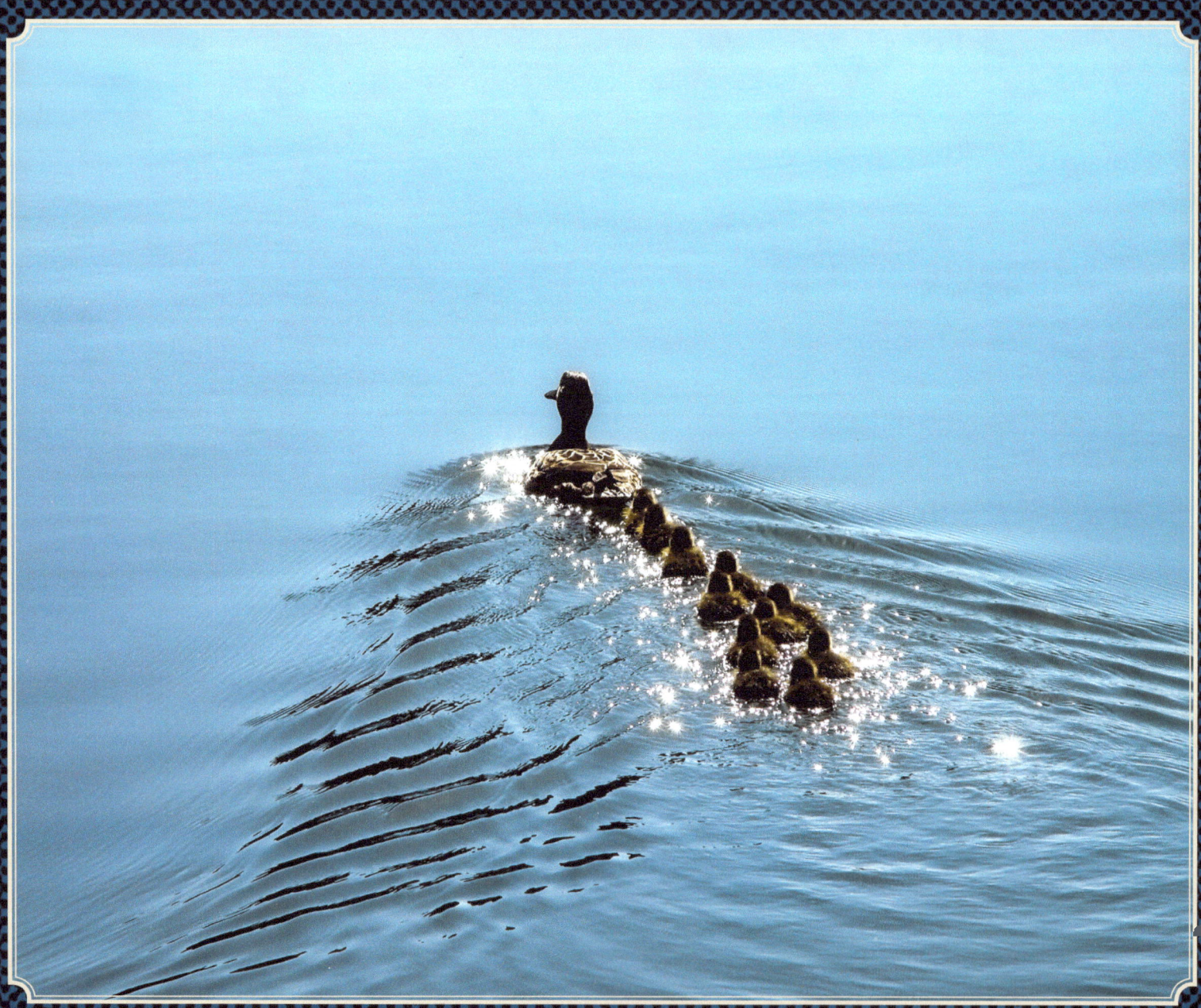

Germani reali
Olbia, Isola Bianca, 2021
Olympus SP565UZ

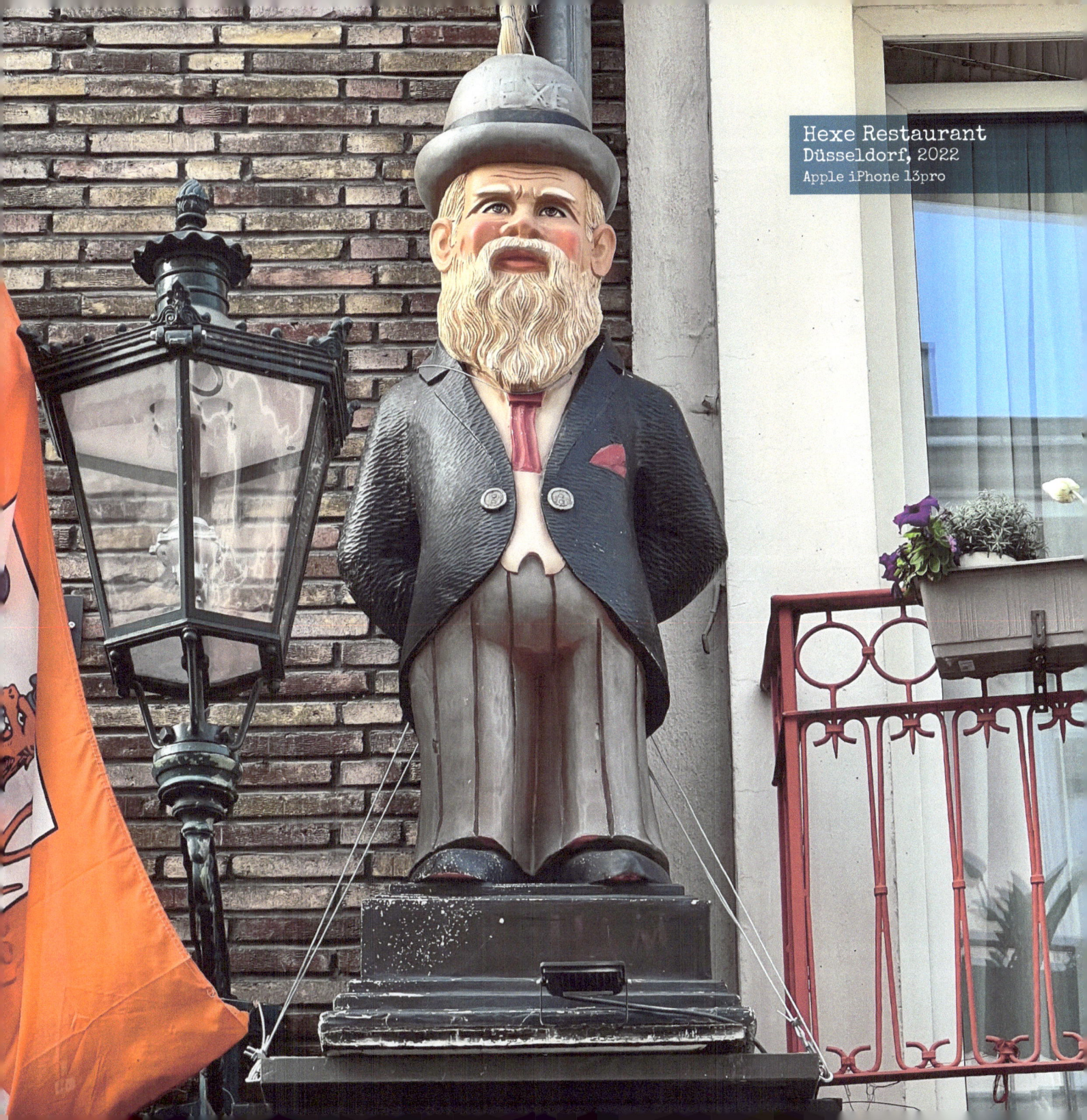

Hexe Restaurant
Düsseldorf, 2022
Apple iPhone 13pro

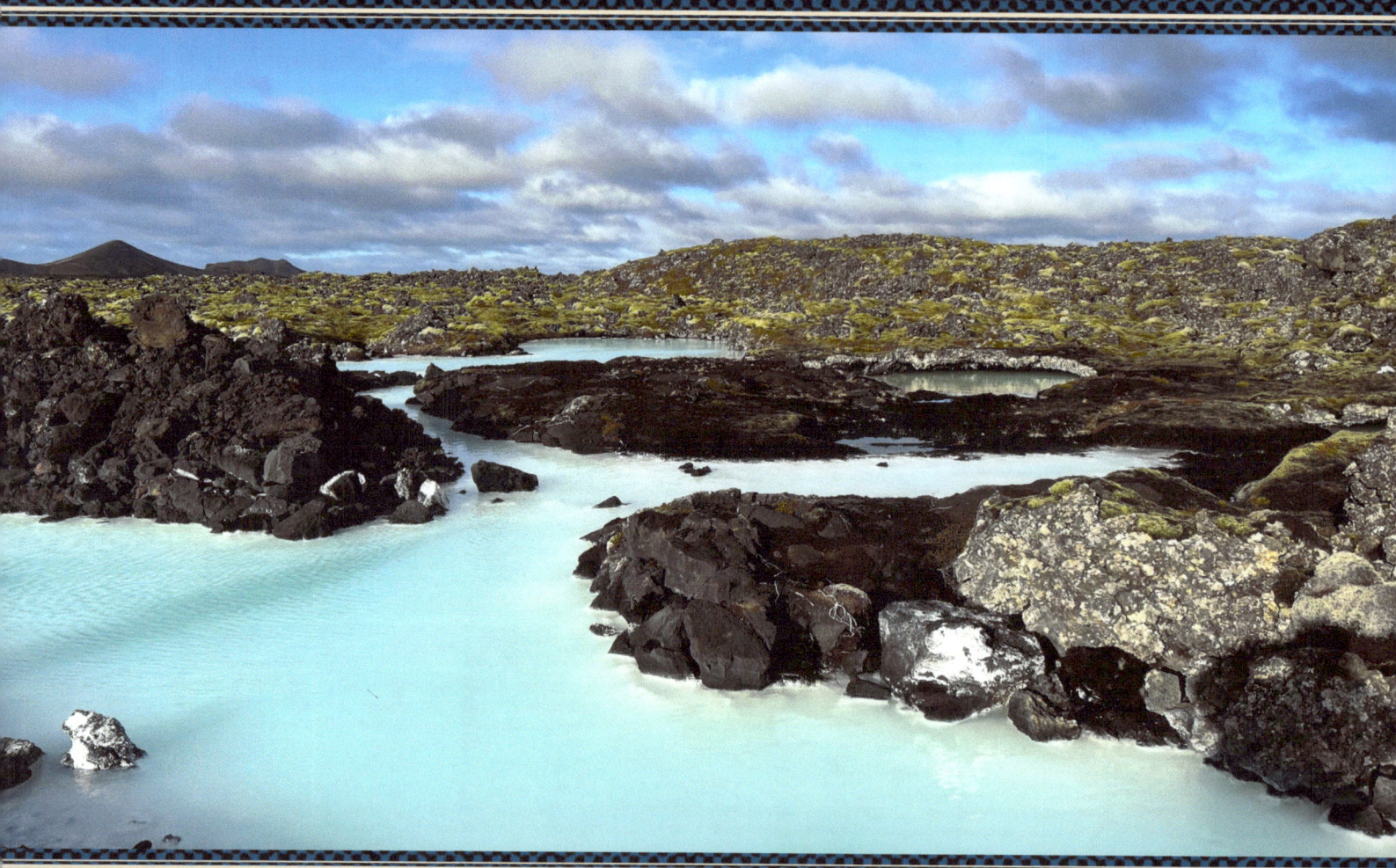

Blue Lagoon
Islanda, 2022
Apple iPhone 13pro

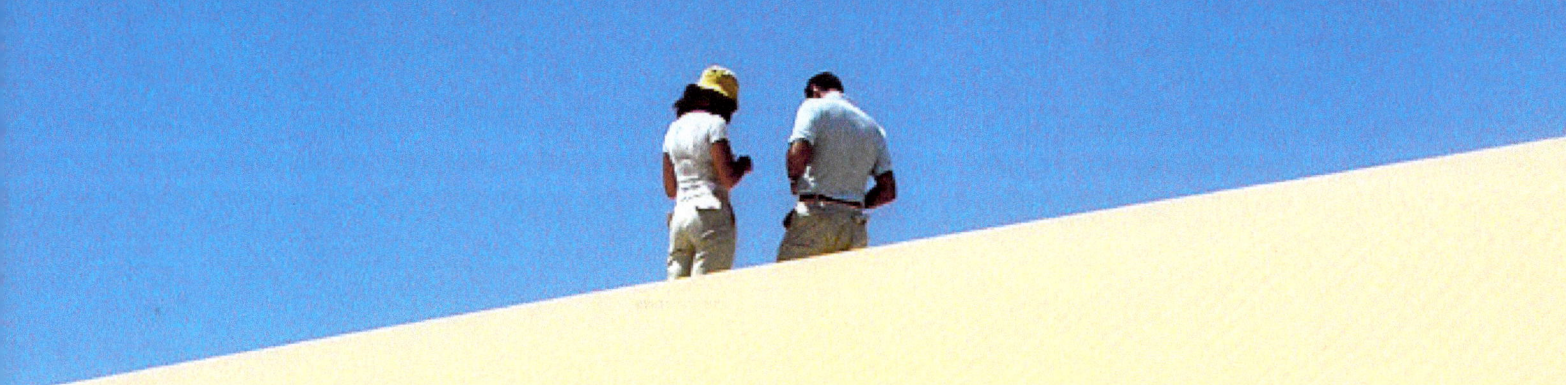

Deserto di Wadi Hitan
Al Fayum, Egitto, 2003
Olympus C3030Z

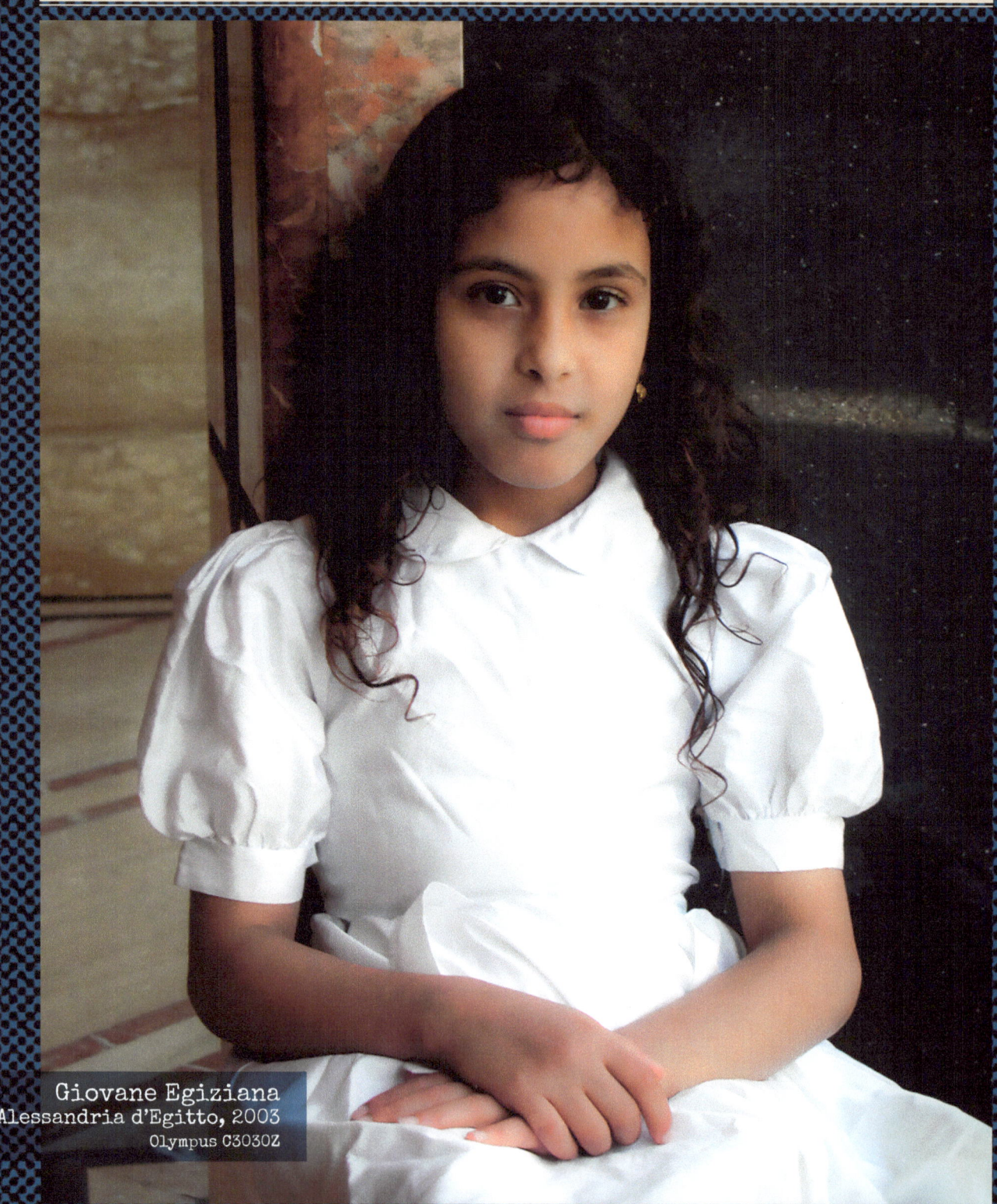

Giovane Egiziana
Alessandria d'Egitto, 2003
Olympus C3030Z

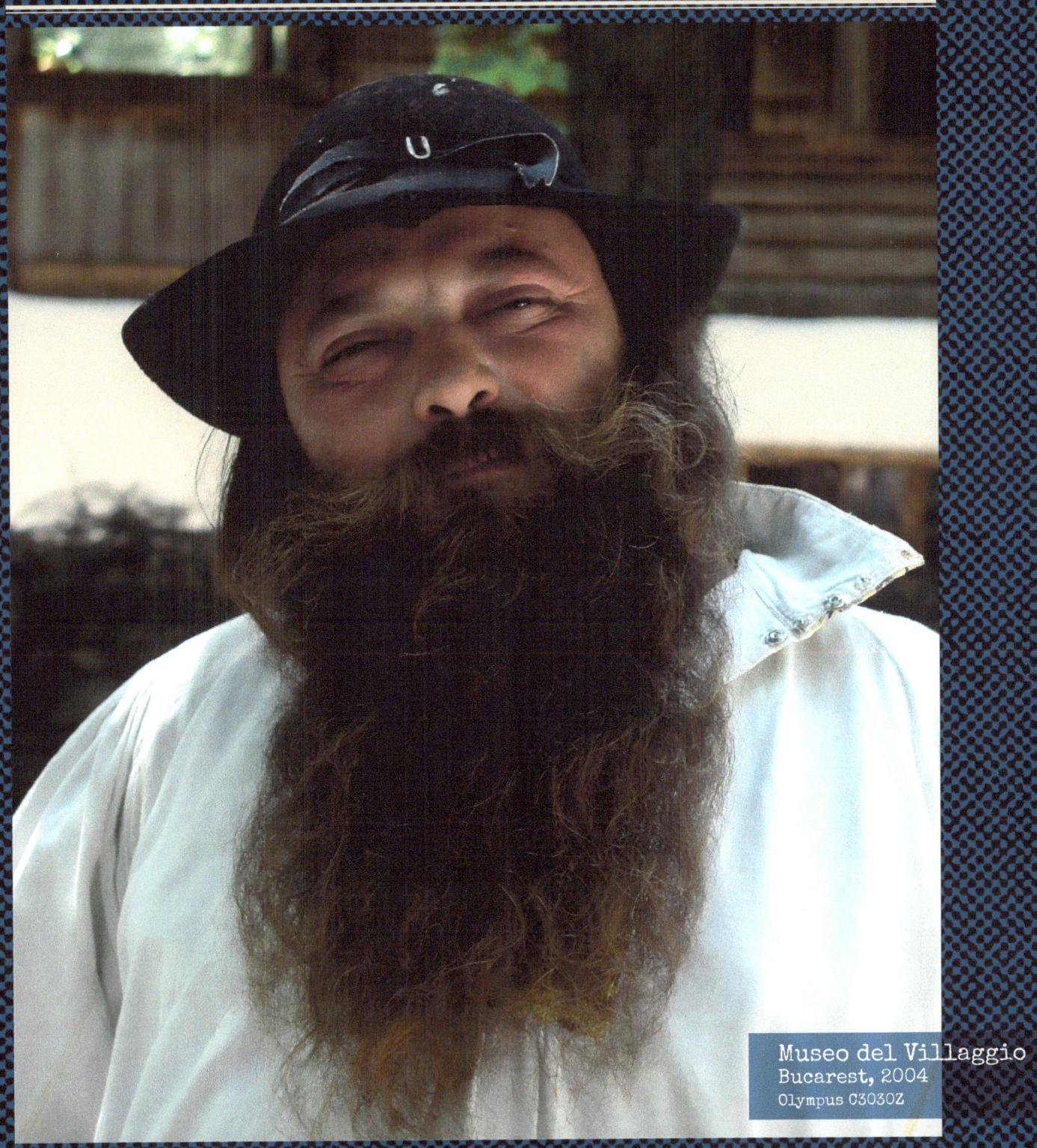

Museo del Villaggio
Bucarest, 2004
Olympus C3030Z

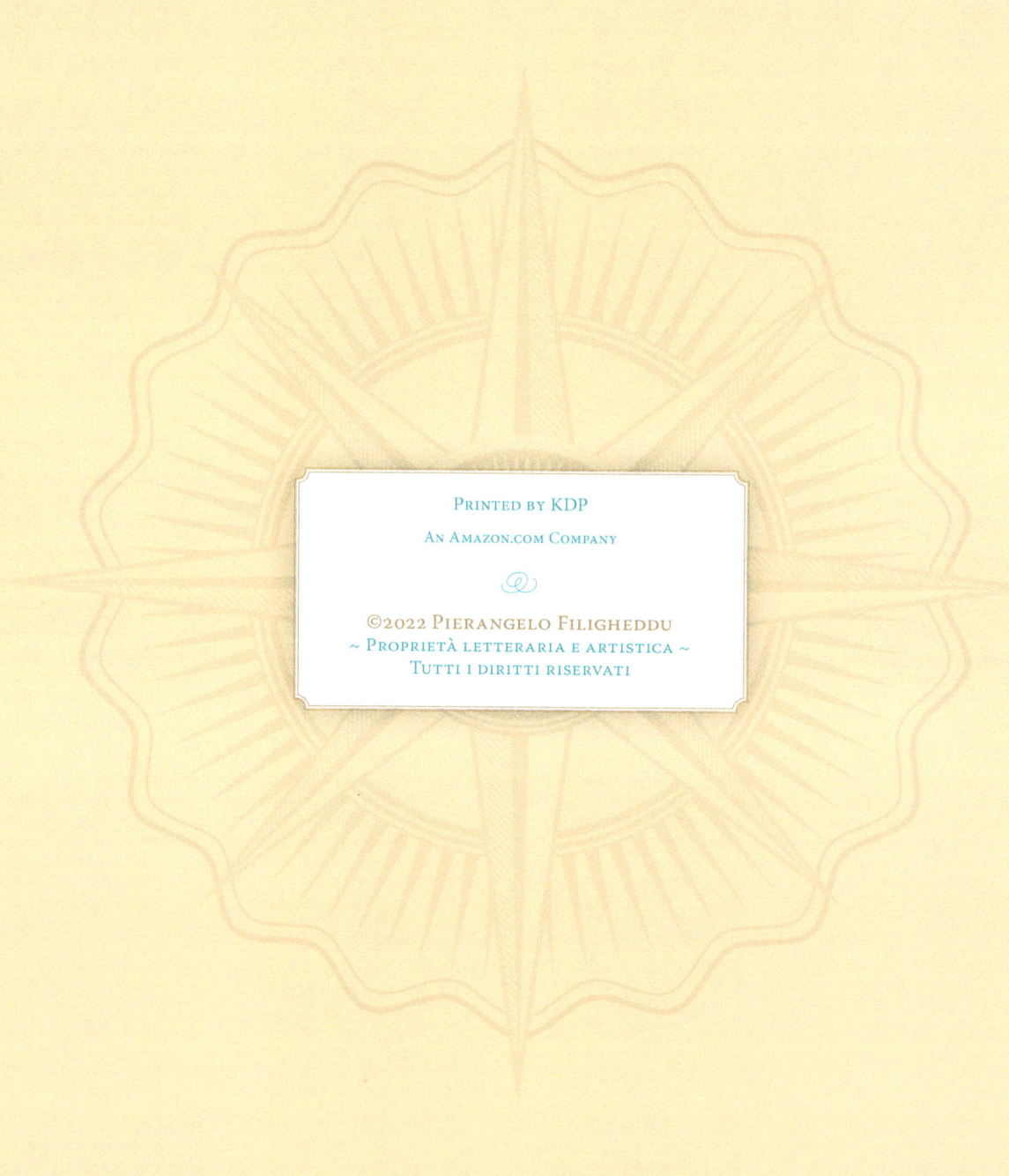

Printed by KDP
An Amazon.com Company

©2022 Pierangelo Filigheddu
~ Proprietà letteraria e artistica ~
Tutti i diritti riservati